Gary Cranford

Sea Dogs
&
Skippers

Sea Dogs & Skippers

Edited by Garry Cranford

Flanker Press Ltd.
St. John's, Newfoundland
2001

National Library of Canada Cataloguing in Publication Data

Sea Dogs and Skippers

Includes bibliographical references and index.
ISBN 1-894463-16-1

1. Shipwrecks–Atlantic Coast (Canada)
2. Shipwrecks–Atlantic Coast (U.S.)   I. Cranford, Garry, 1950-

G525.S42 2001   971.5   C2001-901245-4

PRINTED IN CANADA

First printing July 2001
Second printing May 2003
Third printing April 2004

— FLANKER PRESS LTD. —

P O Box 2522, Stn C,
St. John's, Newfoundland, Canada, A1C 6K1

Toll Free: 1-866-739-4420   Telephone: (709) 739-4477
Facsimile: (709) 739-4420   E-mail: info@flankerpress.com
www.flankerpress.com

Canada

We acknowledge the financial support of the Government of Canada through the Book Publishing Industry Development Program (BPIDP) for our publishing program.

Acknowledgements

Some of these contributors are old "sea dogs" themselves, in terms of their writing experience. Cassie Brown, author of three blockbuster sea stories, opens the book with her examination of the Newfoundland dog myth at the wreck of the SS *Ethie*, a myth that has stoked the imaginations of writers around the world. She is best known for her three classics in maritime history: *Death on the Ice*, *A Winter's Tale*, and *Standing into Danger*. A collection of her short stories, *The Caribou Disaster and other Short Stories* was published a few years ago.

The other lady in this collection is Rosalind (Wareham) Power, author of *A Narrow Passage: Shipwrecks and Tragedies in the St. John's Narrows*, and who brings a personal perspective in that she relates the death of her maternal grandfather, a St. John's harbour pilot.

Rev. John E. Currey is a regular contributor of seafaring tales to the *Downhomer* magazine and author of *Sailors & Their Ships*.

Jack Feltham is author of several books, including *Bonavista Bay Revisited*, *Northeast from Baccalieu*, and *Sealing Steamers*.

Among the other veteran writers of sea stories is the tag team of Frank Galgay and Mike McCarthy, who have written many books on their own and as co-authors. They are widely known for their series *Shipwrecks*, Vol. 1 through 4, and their next co-authored work will be *Olde St. John's*, detailing the history of the great capital city of Newfoundland.

Arden Hall is new to the publishing world as a writer but he is a lover of all Newfoundland and Labrador books. He can be seen every weekend at flea markets in St. John's, Newfoundland, selling and trading old books.

Robert C. Parsons is the admiral of the writing fleet in Newfoundland when it comes to shipwrecks and sea yarns.

He is author of half a dozen books, including *Committed to the Deep, Survive the Savage Sea, Raging Winds...Roaring Sea*, and the soon-to-be-released *Lost at Sea*.

Earl B. Pilgrim is the most popular author in Newfoundland. He is author of perhaps the most talked-about book in Newfoundland, *Curse of the Red Cross Ring*, as well as three other Canadian best-sellers: *Will Anyone Search for Danny?*, *The Price Paid for Charley*, and *Blood on the Hills*.

Retired mariner Captain Joseph Prim and his wealth of information on ships, crews and their captains are well known in Newfoundland. He has worked closely with Frank Galgay and Mike McCarthy on their *Shipwrecks* books and co-authored *The Angry Seas* with Mike McCarthy.

Shannon Ryan is an associate professor in the department of history at Memorial University of Newfoundland and the author of *Fish Out of Water, the Newfoundland Saltfish Trade, 1814-1914*, and *Ice Hunters: A History of Newfoundland Sealing to 1914*, the authoritative text on the history of the sealing industry in Newfoundland.

Clarence Vautier is a young man from the southwest coast of Newfoundland who works on the water. He has written approximately eighty short sea stories not yet published.

Jim Wellman is a retired radio broadcaster, author of *The Fisheries Broadcast*, and most recently *Lighthouse People*, a popular book on the history of lighthouse families in Newfoundland and Labrador.

Garry Cranford is the author or co-author of four books and editor of three others. He is best known for his history of the knockabout schooner *Norma & Gladys*. He is president of Flanker Press Ltd.

Special thanks go out to all of these contributors, as well as to Bruce Ricketts and Dottie Olson for the use of the dog photo featured on the cover.

Contents

The Dog that Wasn't

CASSIE BROWN

The Dog that Wasn't

There's a dog that wasn't, in the wreck of the *Ethie*, which is legendary, for it has been recorded for all time in a Newfoundland folk song, and has its niche in Newfoundland history.

One of Newfoundland's most outstanding seamen, and one of the last of his kind in North America today, is Captain John Gullage, OBE, who was the chief officer of the *Ethie*. As the chief officer, John Gullage considered it his duty to take the risks he did for his captain and his ship. "I was a young man," he said, "and perhaps a little more foolhardy than I am today."

However, about the dog.

According to newspaper reports in a February issue of the *Daily News* in 1920, a few months after the wreck of the *Ethie*, there was a story to the effect that a Newfoundland dog owned by Reuben Decker had swum out and got the line, bringing it to shore, and thus was the factor in getting the people ashore so quickly.

Now, there had been no mention of the dog in the original account given by the survivors, but then there wasn't too much of a story published about the wrecked ship, owing, no doubt, to the fact that the wreck took place on an isolated island, and it was practically a week before news of it reached the capital city. Communications in those days were not as extensive as they are today.

Suddenly, two or three months after the wreck, a new hero is born. A dog had saved nearly a hundred people. Subsequent stories in the *Daily News* revealed that the story had come from the American paper *The Philadelphia Ledger*, and the readers of that paper were already sending contributions for a silver collar for the fearless Newfoundland dog.

It was a great story—a wonderful story. It fired the imagination of the people—it made good copy. So when we interviewed the wonderful Captain Gullage last summer, we said, "...but what about the dog that swam out for the line?"

He said forthrightly, "That's bull! There was no dog." He added grimly, "We were the dogs."

I stuttered, "B-but the newspaper said..."

His voice was firm, decisive, "Dismiss it from your mind, girl. There was no dog."

I was deflated. "For Pete's sake, how did such a rumour start?"

"I'll tell you," he said. "Paddy Burton, our chief engineer, told that story coming through on the train. It was just a story, mind you, told for devilment, but that's how it got started."

It fell neatly into place. In 1919, *The Philadelphia Ledger* had a local correspondent in Curling. A story told jokingly had been taken seriously and sent off to the *Ledger*, which had, without doubt, made excellent reading. The local newspapers got wind of the dog story only when contributions were pouring in to the *Ledger* for the silver collar.

Said Captain Gullage, "I believe they even came to Newfoundland to buy the dog."

I said, "What happened?"

He confessed, "I don't know. Reuben Decker did have a dog, a mongrel dog, but I believe they dug one up somewhere for the Americans." Then he added grimly, "But there was no dog that day. We were the dogs."

So there you have the story of the dog that wasn't.

"Hero" Is A Fake!

CASSIE BROWN

"Hero" Is A Fake!

For years, a legendary Newfoundland dog was reputed to have helped save the lives of the 92 people on the wrecked *Ethie*, as the seas pounded her to pieces, December 10, 1919, at Martin's Point, on Newfoundland's bleak, northwest coast.

The dog was supposedly owned by Reuben Decker, who played a major role in helping to get the people ashore, and his Newfoundland dog is supposed to have swum out in mountainous seas, grabbed a fouled lifeline and brought it to shore.

The story of the dog has been embellished throughout the years, but everyone was firmly convinced it was true, since it was in all the papers, and people in the United States had collected money enough to buy a silver collar for the brave dog.

In an exclusive story to *Woman* (December 1963 issue), Captain John Gullage, OBE, who was then a mate on the

9

Ethie, bluntly stated that there was no Newfoundland dog on the scene to pick up their fouled lifeline. "That is bull! There was no dog. We were the dogs," he said forthrightly.

But even this year, 1964, local writers kept sending in stories to mainland magazines about the Newfoundland dog that saved the wrecked *Ethie's* passengers and crew, so this summer we decided to find the truth of the matter.

We made enquiries while over on the west coast and tracked down Reuben Decker, who is still living, though he is a sick, 70-year-old man today, and we herewith give you his story—the true story of Hero.

It happened on Reuben Decker's twenty-sixth birthday. He and his dog, Wisher, a little yellow crossbreed collie, had just come out of the woods with a load of wood. Wisher was a pet, but Reuben used her for hauling wood, in spite of the fact that there was a law that did not permit dogs to roam because of sheep in the area.

As they came out of the woods, Reuben saw the *Ethie* just as she struck bottom. He didn't know what ship it was, but when he saw her he ran to collect other men and to find ropes and dories to get to the wreck.

Wisher, ever faithful to her master, slipped her harness and tacked after him, and when the men had eventually gathered on the lip of the hill, she was there with them.

The seas were frightful, and Reuben Decker had never seen the like of them before or since, and after about an hour and a half, they eventually did hook the lifeline from the water and began to pull it in. Wisher grabbed the rope, too, because her master held it.

Well, all the people on board the *Ethie* were saved, and Reuben Decker recalls that his skin was burned off his face with the frost, and for days he had ten or eleven people staying in his house. They had no place to sleep but on the floor.

Life returned to normal when the survivors left, and none was more surprised than Reuben the next summer to learn that Wisher was credited with saving the lives of the people of the *Ethie*.

To his consternation, he learned that there was a delegation of people coming from St. John's to present Wisher with a valuable collar for her intelligence and bravery. Reuben Decker denied emphatically that his dog had done anything, but suddenly, nobody believed him.

Quite suddenly, many people were interested in Wisher, the little yellow crossbreed collie, and no matter how often he told them the truth, he simply wasn't believed. Thinking back over it, Reuben Decker says ruefully, "If I had a mind to tell a lie, I'd have got a big price for Wisher."

There was to be a party for Reuben and Wisher, in Bonne Bay. Plans had been made for a big garden party with Reuben and Wisher as guests of honour, and quite resigned to it all, Reuben put his dog in a small boat, and they made it down the coast to Bonne Bay.

At the party, there was Judge Kent from St. John's, and many other important guests on board the coastal boat, who had come on the trip especially to witness the event. In a special ceremony, Judge Kent presented him with a plush-lined box containing a leather collar with a silver plate attached by chains. On it was inscribed HERO.

Reuben Decker had to accept it, but he told the judge and his friends that Wisher had done nothing to deserve it, and they still didn't believe him. Reuben and Wisher were invited aboard the ship as special guests.

The policeman of Bonne Bay had warned Reuben that if Wisher was ever found "on the run" she would be shot just like any other dog, and knowing of the restriction placed on dogs, Judge Kent further awarded Wisher the special privilege of roaming around free.

The garden party was a great success, and little Wisher was the star of the show. Lots of people wanted to buy her, but the most persuasive was a William Orum of Saint John, New Brunswick. He gave Reuben Decker $30.00 for Wisher and became the owner of the now-famous dog, because, he said, he wanted to take her around on exhibition.

Too late, a William Prebble of Bonne Bay offered to take Reuben and the dog around on an expenses-paid tour. Reuben's pet now belonged to a stranger. Said he, "Thirty dollars was a lot of money those days, and I was a poor man."

It is from this point that the legend of the Newfoundland dog "Hero" begins. Reuben still had the silver collar, and three months after he had sold Wisher, the man who bought her turned up asking for the collar, and Reuben sold it for another thirty dollars.

He never did see or hear of Wisher again, but soon after, he received newspaper pictures of "Hero" the dog who saved the lives of the people on the wrecked *Ethie*, but it wasn't any picture of the little yellow crossbreed collie, but a big black Newfoundland dog.

So a harmless story told perhaps jokingly, perhaps in earnest, brought into being a fake "Hero." It is logical to conclude that the man from New Brunswick decided that the huge, gentle Newfoundland dog made the story sound much more authentic than the little yellow collie, since Newfoundland dogs are famed for doing just such heroic things. He had bought the collar, and apparently he had bought a Newfoundland dog to go with it, pawning the creature off as "Hero."

While such legends about our own breed of dog does warm the cockles of the heart, it doesn't alter the fact that it was a lie from beginning to end. Hero was a figment of an overripe imagination.

Editor's Note: Eighty years after the wreck of the *Ethie*, the leather collar and two medals surfaced at the Roadside Diner in Wrangell, Alaska. The owners, Dick and Dottie Olson, were cleaning out the premises when they found the artifacts. Eventually, they contacted Mr. Bruce Ricketts at www.mysteriesofcanada.com who in turn made arrangements for the collar and medals to be displayed at the Newfoundland Museum, St. John's. Information on how the collar and medals travelled from New Brunswick to Alaska is available on Mr. Ricketts's Web site. Without drawing any conclusions that might complicate matters, it is interesting that a photograph of an unidentified dog was found with the artifacts and can be seen on the Web site, and it looks to be a dead ringer for a cross between a collie and a Newfoundland!

The collar and medals at the Newfoundland Museum are beautiful artifacts. On the collar are fastened two starry crosses on either side of a plate with the word Hero. An attached medallion with the number 92 on one side has inscribed on the back, Presented to Hero by the Starry Cross of Philadelphia, PA, in token of appreciation for his rescue of 92 souls from the Ethie on December 10th 1919.

The second medallion attached to the collar is a cross of sterling silver. It reads, Presented to HERO by the sick soldiers of Camp Hill Hospital, Halifax, NS, May 7th, 1923.

Clearly, the "man from New Brunswick" or his successor continued to reap the benefits of a Newfoundland dog scam for years after the wreck of the *Ethie*.

Now that the truth about the Newfoundland dog myth has been laid to rest, the question has to be asked, "What ever happened to Wisher?"

The Wreck of the Edward VII

GARRY CRANFORD

The Wreck of the Edward VII

"In the last day aboard the *Edward VII*, the crewmen were fully aware of their impending doom. The weather was continuously bad, but within the last few hours the glass had gone down so low as to indicate an even more fierce storm was coming, and soon. They knew that unless some ship picked them up, this was literally their last day."—Mate Dan Vey

In the age of schooners in Newfoundland, every fall, in late November, an armada of small- and medium-sized vessels left St. John's for their home ports. They had delivered all their codfish to the Water Street merchants, and were returning home with their supplies of rough grub for the winter and fishing materials for spring start-up. From the time since she was built in Long Beach, Trinity Bay in 1901, the schooner *Edward VII*, 45 tons, had made this annual pilgrimage.

Throughout his career, Captain Wilson Vey was a Labrador man for 42 summers, a Newfoundlander who prosecuted the Labrador codfishery. He took over the family's 60-foot schooner from his father and continued the family tradition of fishing the Labrador, in one year joining up to nine other schooners that sailed from his hometown of Long Beach, Trinity Bay.

On the finest kind of a Saturday morning, November 25, 1933, the *Edward VII* moved away from her moorings and slipped through the St. John's Narrows. Captain Wilson Vey and Mate Daniel Vey (the skipper's brother), along with two crew and five passengers, expected a pleasant run home, though it was slow going because of little wind. Another Trinity Bay schooner, the *Jack Tar*, left St. John's at the same time.

The glass began to fall, and before they got through Baccalieu Tickle, the crew of the *Edward VII* could see the wind breaking the clouds abroad. They were about four miles out in Trinity Bay from Baccalieu when the wind chopped from the northwest, and it came on to blow hard. The wind was now in their teeth and increasing to hurricane force.

Aboard the vessel were the following men: Captain Wilson Vey of Long Beach; Mate Daniel Vey of Long Beach; Johnny Brown of Hatchet Cove; Llewellyn Barfitt of Long Beach; James Gosse of Long Beach; George Smith of Island Cove; Edmund Allen Lambert of Hatchet Cove; Josiah Drover of Hodge's Cove; John Barfitt of Long Beach.

With all the canvas except the foresail taken down, they thought they might make headway across to Trinity or some other safe harbour on the north side of the bay. When he saw they weren't making any progress, Captain Vey hove the vessel around to let her drive down on a retreat course through Baccalieu Tickle once again, thinking he might find a sheltered place to drop anchor.

Unfortunately, when they were broadside to Grate's Cove, the foresail blew right out of its ropes. To regain some control over their drift, the crew unstopped the mainsail, but a sea immediately broke into it, taking it out over the rail, bursting it abroad as it went. Next, the jumbo cracked off five or six feet down from the top clew. There was nothing to do now but put her out to sea to clear Baccalieu.

It was just after dark when the vessel cleared the island and drove out east. Out in the lun of Baccalieu, Captain Vey ordered the men, "Bar up the cabin and forecastle doors, and batten down the hatches, because we're going to be in for a hard night."

It came on freezing now, and with the frost came snow dwighs. The salt spray was frozen as far as fifteen feet up the mainboom, where the ice was an inch thick. Their boat was lashed to the deck, but its ballast of spray and ice also kept it solidly pinned down. They were going off fast, and the skipper prepared the men for what might happen. "If we hold on going out east, we'll see no land tomorrow morning."

To slow the schooner's drift away from Newfoundland, the crew tied several rubber tires together with heavy cordage and tossed them overboard to act as a sea anchor. This made things worse, because the drag affected the buoyancy of the schooner, deadening her progress, causing the waves to break at her stern and go over her head with even greater force and frequency than before. Captain Vey had the crew cut it away to let her go on her own and run clear of the seas.

That night, with the seas breaking over the little vessel, Captain Vey spent an hour up on the maingaff, watching the rolls and breaks in the seas coming behind. If possible, he would caution the man tied to the wheel to brace himself as the worst waves broke over the stern and rushed headlong, cleaning out everything ahead of it.

19

At midnight, the vessel shipped a sea which carried away all the bulwarks and several drums of oil stacked on deck. This made it very difficult to get around. A couple of the barrels rolled aft, where Mate Dan Vey was frantically beating ice off the wheel and bar, which were very badly iced up. With an iron grip on the wheel chain, Dan barely escaped being washed overboard. Instead, the waves tumbled over him, and while submerged, he felt one of the loose fuel drums roll over his legs, but luckily he was uninjured.

The crew could not believe that all this happened on the first day out!

Sunday morning broke with a beautiful sunrise and clear skies. The wind veered a little farther northward with no snow, but did it ever blow! This was very dangerous, since the spray iced up the vessel so much that she was nearly decked in the water. As the sun rose higher in the sky, the air began to warm, and the crew managed to chop and beat off some of the ice.

Next, they patched enough canvas to keep the vessel under steerage-way. After a long while, they were able to hoist a double-reef mainsail and staysail, and since the winds were lighter, they were able to lay to, headed into the wind. All of a sudden, in the heavy swell, the mainboom swung out hard, breaking into two pieces.

It was now Sunday evening, and two steamships came in view, only half a mile away, but despite the schooner's distress signal, they passed on by.

It was relatively calm, but the barometer began to rise, and the skipper was greatly relieved. It meant that the wind would veer around in an easterly direction, forcing the schooner back towards land. This raised the spirits of the crew as they began the task of repairing the mainboom. They laid the two pieces along the deck and reinforced it with a length of gaff, shaped flat on one side with an axe. They bored holes through the gaff and into the pieces of boom and drove in twelve-inch spikes. Repositioning the mainboom, they bent on the little scrap of sail they had left and hoisted the remains of the jumbo. As the night wore on, the wind increased, with blinding sleet and snow, and the schooner ran before it, moving closer to land.

Monday dawned a coppery red, with a blinding snow-storm freshening up, causing them to run northwest toward land until late in the afternoon. The seas ran high, so they took in their precious scraps of canvas.

Meanwhile, the Newfoundland Department of Marine and Fisheries issued an order: "Notify all passing steamers to look out for mising schooners *Jack Tar* and *Edward VII*."

In the evening, the curse of bad luck revisited the schooner, as the wind veered to west-northwest, forcing the schooner out into open sea again.

Tuesday—day four—was much the same, witnessing the vessel drifting away from land. In the evening, the *Edward VII* was becalmed in a heavy swell, with winds blowing around the perimeter. The seas, behaving like a tide rip, took turns breaking in over the port and starboard sides. There was no pattern to the sea's pounding from all quarters, and the battering caused her seams to open up so much that, from this time onward, the pumps had to be manned at all times.

At a later date, Skipper Vey wrote, "This was one of the worst days we had while adrift. According to the high seas that were running, I think we must have been somewhere near the Virgin Rocks, and the seas began to tell on our little vessel as she became leaky and her seams began to open, which caused us to keep the pumps working all the time. No doubt we had a good crew. Five of the men were passengers who went to St. John's with us to get their winter supplies. If it had-n't been for the passengers we had on board, I don't think our small crew would have lasted long enough to keep her afloat."

The wind veered to the northwest, and the vessel began running southerly, before the wind, when a big passenger ship came in view. She was so close the crew could see men walking about on the deck as its three stacks billowed smoke, but they were not close enough to read the name on her hull. It came to within half a mile of the little schooner, but despite all efforts to signal and attract its attention, she gave them no assistance and passed by, on her route to some safe port in Europe.

The little schooner's crew could not know it, but at noon-time, Captain Stanley Barbour took the SS *Cape Agulhas* through the St. John's Narrows on a rescue mission. Minister John G. Stone of the Department of Marine and Fisheries had instructed Barbour to search the waters adjacent to the Avalon Peninsula for signs of two schooners, the *Jack Tar* and the *Edward VII*. The *Jack Tar* had since arrived safely at Hillview, Trinity Bay, so the steamer's spotters quickly focused their attention on the four horizons for a schooner with Captain Vey and his crew aboard.

Captain Barbour set down a course to methodically cover a specific grid of ocean waters. He left at noon and headed east-southeast for a distance of 80 miles, until he was within 20 miles of the Virgin Rocks.

Later in the day, through the scattered snow dwighs, Captain Vey saw several ships that passed on the horizon. All they saw was the smoke from their stacks, about eight or ten miles away. Unfortunately, the SS *Cape Agulhas* was not one of them.

With another long and stormy night coming on and no fire to dry or warm themselves, the crew began to think very hard of the ships that passed them.

Water was now coming down through the deck seams, and when Captain Vey went to survey the forecastle, it was a sorry-looking sight. The hardy men were nearly broken down, some of them on their knees, praying. Captain Vey joined in and asked God to watch over them and guard them through the night.

Years later, Captain Vey believes their prayers were answered: in due time. He recalled, "Poor Uncle Lew had the wheel this night. I got up on the maingaff and held on to the halyards of the mainsail. I used to watch those big seas when they'd come and break. I'd say, 'Uncle Lew, watch out, boy. Hold on!' He used to reeve his two hands through the wheel, and when the sea would break, it broke right down on top of him. We had him tied on, and he floated right up. We had the end of the mainsheet tied to him, so if he washed overboard, we could haul him in."

Wednesday the twenty-ninth was day five on the water. The vessel drifted along, but the crew saw nothing in sight. They were getting short of fresh water, so they put themselves on voluntary rations of one cup of tea during the day and one at night. Although they were feeling very thirsty, they could not use up the water. However, they did manage to get some fluids in the juice from apples. The couple of times they scraped up snow from the decks proved to be useless, since it was contaminated with salt spray. Their wood was getting scarce, since they didn't stow in very much at St. John's. They had expected a short run to their home port. To boil their kettle for their two daily cups of tea, they cut up parts of the vessel.

Captain Barbour worked the steamer on a course along an 85-mile line, northeast-1/2-north. He said, "The wind was blowing a strong breeze from the northwest with heavy seas, which were continually boarding the ship and running out through the scuppers." At 7:00 P.M. he turned the steamer to the southeast.

By the next day, the *Cape Agulhas* had travelled to a position 100 miles east-southeast of St. John's. Early in the morning, Thursday, Captain Barbour decided to try the last leg of his search. He set a course to west-northwest and steamed all day, until 4:00 P.M., to within 20 miles of Sugarloaf, near St. John's. In all, the ship had steamed 300 miles. There was no schooner or identifiable wreckage to be seen, only busy steamers rushing headlong to their international ports. But the *Edward VII* was still out there, the crew desperately clinging to life and sanity.

At five o'clock, just in time for a homemade hot supper, the *Cape Agulhas* returned to St. John's. The search had proven futile, and the crew gave up all expectations of finding the schooner. The *Evening Telegram* reported that she had searched "the ocean within a radius of 100 miles of St. John's without seeing any trace of the vessel."

On Thursday, the thirtieth, all day and all night another storm of wind and snow howled down from the skies, and the pumps never stopped. They had to be manned during all shifts, and not once did anyone refuse to do his part. The drinking water was used up, and to keep warm the crew burned pork and rubber tires.

While the crew of the *Cape Agulhas* departed for their heated homes and boarding houses with their dry, warm feather beds, the crew on the *Edward VII* wondered how much longer they could last in the extreme weather. The crew spent very little time on deck and at the pumps, and they stayed in the forecastle. Though sheltered from the wind, they were in great mental distress. One poor fellow, Uncle Jim, the skipper's uncle by marriage, didn't get out of his bunk at all. Every now and then he'd moan, "Oh my, I'll never see Maxie again." Maxie was the grandson he had reared. The poor old man was despondent. John Barfitt was a comfort to the men; every day he would lead the men in prayers, a role which came naturally to him, as he was the lay reader for his church.

With the schooner not found and all hope given up by the authorities, the residents of Long Beach and nearby communities were very disheartened. There was only one thing to do now. Even though there were no bodies for the granny-women to wash, dress, and lay out in their homemade coffins, it was time to hold a service, a funeral service for nine. Hymns and a sermon suitable for a burial at sea were chosen, and everyone trudged up the lane to the church door, heavy of heart.

Such a blow to a small community was devastating, considering that many of the men were related. Wilson and Daniel Vey were brothers. Llewellyn Barfitt and his brother John were their brothers-in-law, and James Gosse was their uncle by marriage. To take these beloved, hard-working and good-living men out of such a small place seemed a tragedy beyond comprehension.

The hymns were sung and the sermon spoken, but there was no sense of peace. Without the tangible trappings of a funeral service, a proper wake to say one's last goodbyes, the procession to the graveyard and the ritual lowering of coffins, there could be no sense of closure.

But there was one holdout. Skipper Bill Vey refused to go along with the others. Bill Vey was blind, but in his mind's eye he could visualize the crew, suffering but alive, tossing on the winds. Bill Vey was Wilson's father, and he had great faith in the little schooner and his son's ability to bring his crew and passengers back home to their families.

Captain Bill Vey knew the schooner well, so he thought. She had been built in 1901 by Joseph Samson, who was one handy fellow when it came to fastening planks to ribs. Fifteen years later, another renowned shipbuilder in the area, Kenneth Frampton, had rebuilt her at White Rock.

Bill Vey probably felt that nothing could dislodge the planks from her frame. Sure, the vessel had been built and rebuilt by the best. Though she was more than thirty years old, she was more than a match for the gales.

On Friday and Saturday—days seven and eight—the winds were moderate, so Wilson Vey put up his rag sails and let the vessel head south. There was a bit of hope on Saturday, when they spotted two steamers about two or three miles away, but spirits faded as these ships took no notice and dipped below the horizon, oblivious to the desperate plight of the schooner's crew.

They saw nothing more until Sunday evening, about six o'clock, when they glimpsed a light ahead. They tossed more kerosene and old rubber boots into their homemade flare, which made a light that could be seen for a long distance, but the vessel passed on. Their hopes of being picked up began to look very grim as the schooner continued disintegrating, and the men were struggling at the pumps. Their efforts were futile.

It was only by the grace of God that they were alive and the schooner afloat.

Captain Vey recalled that on the evening of the ninth day, just about dusk, Uncle George Smith was forward, looking out. Mate Dan Vey was also on deck, at the pumps. Vey was himself at the wheel, and there were times he didn't care if the sea washed over him or not. He was that far gone, with no sleep, for nine days and nights. The ship was in a terrible state, nearly sunk. The water had come up over the floor in the forecastle.

Captain Vey heard George Smith shout from the bow, "I think I see a light ahead! A long way away!"

Then, not so certain, "I don't know if it was a light or what it was. It *looked* like a light."

The vessel went down in a swell, and darkness closed in around it. When she came up on top of the swell, George bawled out, "I just seen it again!"

Mate Dan Vey spotted the light at the same time.

It had to be a ship, thought Captain Vey.

Strengthened with hope, their hearts pumped new energy into their legs and arms, the crew set about refueling the flare. This was actually a fuel cask that hadn't washed overboard a week earlier, found jammed between the counter and the wheel. Captain Vey had brought the salvaged drum forward and lashed it to the mainmast. Taking out a marlin pike, he had punched a hole near the bottom of the can, to let the kerosene oil drain away. The rim on the top of the barrel made a wide, shallow pan, and every night, the crew kept it supplied with kerosene, topped up with chunks of salt pork, which would flare high into the night sky when it ignited. Other times it was fueled with oakum. This time, Skipper Vey took no chances. He doubled up on the pork.

He recalled, "That's what this steamer saw! The captain said he saw this flare-up about twenty miles away!"

The *Edward VII* was drifting away on a southerly course, and the crew could see the cargo vessel's port and starboard lights coming right for them, right on their line of drift. She came alongside and shone their powerful searchlights.

Captain Vey shouted above the wind, "We are in a sinking condition!"

He repeated this several times, but there was no answer. Ten minutes later, his heart sank as the steamer parted from the schooner. She was about four or five miles away when Captain Vey saw her change position, the port lights coming into view. "She's turning around!"

Captain Vey recalled the joyous change in fortune. "She turned right around and came right back on us again, where she had left. The wind was gone now, moderate, but there was a big swell on. If you went down in one of them big swells, you wouldn't see the steamer, right alongside. By and by you would come up and there she would be, broadside with the swell."

The little schooner was on its last legs. Before abandoning ship, Captain Vey checked the water in the cabins and the forecastle. Despite the constant pumping, there was half a foot of water fore and aft. It was time to go.

There was one thing the crew had done correctly. When they left St. John's they had securely lashed a new boat down to the deck so well that nine days of pounding waves could not dislodge it. Throughout the whole ordeal it had stayed put, and now it was their lifeboat to the steamer. With considerable difficulty in the swelling seas, they got it positioned for several men to jump in, and then lowered it overboard. All nine got aboard, just as they were, with only the clothes on their backs.

Up and down the swells, the men rowed their open boat around their schooner, up to the bigger vessel. They had to be nimble on the water, careful not to get too close, for fear that in rolling broadside to the wind while sheltering the little boat, they might strike its gunwale and send the nine drifters to the bottom.

The crew of the steamer threw ropes across the little boat for the men to grab and tie around their waists. This was difficult due to the cold and wet weather and the heavy rubber clothes that made moving almost impossible. The crew also dropped ladders down the side of the large vessel and, using their ropes, Vey and his crew pulled the boat towards the ladders. It was a tricky thing, to grab one, because it had to be done at the right moment. If anyone grabbed a ladder when she was rolling down, he would get a dunking, but grabbing it on an uproll meant he was lifted along with the ladder, away from the water. If a man lost his grip on a ladder, he could be hauled aboard by the rope tied around his waist.

"As it was night," Wilson Vey wrote, "this made it very difficult for us to abandon our waterlogged vessel. Leaving her in our own small boat was indeed very dangerous in such weather, but we had to do it. On reaching the side of the steamer, ropes were thrown down to each man to catch, and a ladder was hanging over the side in which every man took his turn, leaving one man, Llewellyn Barfitt, in the boat to fasten on a few little things we saved and hauled up on board. As he reached the deck, he fell exhausted and was taken to the sick room and cared for by the ship's first mate who was acting as doctor. Once on board we thanked God for his great mercy towards us in bringing us through."

The vessel that had spotted them was the *Maine*, a Danish ship carrying potash to the United States. She had been having a hard time of it herself in that brutal storm, and, ironically, they had just been reminded over the wireless to keep an eye out for distressed vessels. Third Officer Alex G. Meyer was the first to spot the kerosene and pork flare aboard the *Edward VII*. He had immediately reported his sighting to Captain Hausen, who turned the vessel on a course to the schooner.

With everyone safely aboard, the *Maine* swung away from the little boat and the sinking schooner. On deck, there were about forty sailors, and none but the captain and first officer could speak English.

The first officer came along, asking, "Who is the skipper among you?"

Someone pointed to Wilson Vey. "There's the skipper."

"Come along with me," he said. "The captain wants to talk to you."

Vey went up to the chart room on the bridge and met Captain Hausen, who cordially asked, "Are you all safe?"

"Yes, Captain. Thank God we're all safe."

"It was quite a job. Where are you from?"

"Newfoundland."

"You were out in all this storm?" asked Hausen.

"Yes," Wilson said, "we were out in all this storm."

The captain of the steamer couldn't believe it. He thought about the little schooner. At the height of the storm, his own vessel had been drifting broadside all day, and he thought she would not survive. A big sea had caught the *Maine* on the bow and caused the vessel to swivel aft, damaging her steering gear. All day Sunday, she would roll down forty-five degrees until her bridge was underwater. The three lifeboats on the windward side were smashed, and the big oak doors on the bridge were cracked and pushed inward. All the sleeping quarters below were flooded.

The vessel was en route to North Carolina with a load of fertilizer. The engineers had gotten the steering gear cleared up, and they had been underway again. This was becoming quite an adventure for Captain Hausen. It was the first trip to Wilmington for the *Maine*, and he had never effected a rescue involving as many people as were aboard the little schooner.

Skipper Vey asked, "Captain, what are we going to do about her? We're supposed to sink her in case she is a menace to some ship." .

"Is there much water in her?" the captain inquired.

"Yes," Vey said, "it's six inches up over the cabin and forecastle floors."

Captain Hausen decided not to ram the vessel, as it was about to sink any second, especially now that the pumps had stopped. Ramming it might cause one of her masts to come in over the rail of the big ship and cause more damage.

After they were straightened away, the captain asked Skipper Vey and the crew, "I guess you would like to send a message to your relatives?"

Vey answered for all. "Yes, Captain, I would."

The captain had a good idea the crew were curious as to how far off shore they had been when they were rescued. "Where do you think you are?" he asked.

Vey answered. "I don't know. We had a log out, but we were going around the compass. One day we went one way, the next day we went another."

They were standing before the chart table. "Where do you think the nearest Marconi is?"

"Probably Cape Race."

"Yes," the captain replied, "you are handy about right." He plotted their current position relative to Newfoundland and determined that the schooner was picked up 300 miles southeast of Cape Race.

Of course, that was only part of the story. That was the straight-line distance from Cape Race. They had left St. John's farther north, and had added hundreds of additional miles, criss-crossing their own wakes as the winds changed and blew them to all points of the compass. Captain Vey asked that the message be sent to Cape Race, where the Marconi station could pick it up and forward it to the Department of Marine Fisheries in St. John's.

The official message to the Minister of Marine and Fisheries was received at 3:00 A.M. on Monday morning, in time for the news to break in the St. John's daily newspapers.

In Long Beach, Trinity Bay, Postmistress Fanny Vey heard the good news clicking out on the telegraph. "Crew of *Edward VII* found. All hands safe."

Fanny's husband George was sitting at the table for lunch. He grabbed the closest thing he could use as a white flag, ran

31

up the beach like a town crier, shouting, "They're safe! They're safe!"

Two hours after the rescue, the gale forecast by the bottomed-out glass struck the vessel. "The nose of the ship seemed to go down forever," wrote Mate Dan Vey. "Even the seams between the molding seemed to froth."

Despite the driving seas that night, the schooner's crew had comfortable quarters, two to a room. Captain Wilson Vey, on the other hand, slept on a big chesterfield up against a wall in the salon. Curious about the ship's behaviour in the seas they were experiencing, he knelt up on the chesterfield and peered out one of the portholes. The vessel was staggering headlong into the troughs, and when she did she vibrated as the big propeller rose clear of the water behind her. She was going at reduced speed, taking about eight hours to do twenty-five miles.

He remarked on the stormy conditions. Captain Hausen declared, "You just made it. This storm was brewing, and if you were out in it you would not have seen home again."

Captain Vey kept his concerns, that they were not home yet, to himself.

This new storm lasted for their first three days aboard the *Maine*. They were driven another 300 miles out into the Atlantic. It would take another eight days—twenty since they left St. John's—before the crew would see land again.

When the storm abated, the air warmed and the seas became smooth. Approaching the Carolina coast, the crew of the freighter called the schoonermen on deck to witness a lightship, moored off shore, about fifteen miles out. "She was lit up like a diamond," recalls Captain Vey.

The freighter proceeded across the bay to a river mouth and anchored for the convenience of the customs officers.

The freighter was down by the head, and for two days the Newfoundlanders worked at clearing the chain lockers of water. The covers used to protect the chain pipes had been smashed off by the stormy seas, and the vessel had taken on nineteen tons of seawater.

On December 13, with her head up a bit more, the vessel was escorted by a pilot boat that took her up a long, dredged channel to the city of Wilmington. What appeared to be a channel was actually the Cape Fear River, the principal waterway of North Carolina.

When docked, the crew uncovered the donkeys and rigged out the derricks to unload the cargo of fertilizer. It looked like sawdust, but it was white and loose. A huge tub would swing out, go down in the hold and, when filled, the men would hoist it up and swing it into a holding bin on the pier.

Captain Vey watched this bustle of activity from the bridge, marvelling at the industry. There was a line of black longshoremen with wheelbarrows coming to the chute to take away the fertilizer. He had never seen a black man before. As the line of workers struggled with their barrows, they sang what sounded to Captain Vey like sea shanties. At lunchtime, he observed the men's wives bringing down their lunches. He was told that they had docked near an area in the city called by the most uncomplimentary name Niggertown.

While their men ate lunch, the women sometimes busied themselves nearby, in a swampy area filled with old woods growth, where they gathered up dried sticks and twigs in their aprons to carry back home.

As soon as the Newfoundlanders were able to go ashore, a newspaperman showed up for a report on the men's ordeal at sea. Captain Vey was well prepared for this. While waiting at dockside, he had borrowed an exercise book from one of the *Maine's* crew and made notes from memory. The following morning, they were given a newspaper with the full account of the wreck of the *Edward VII*.

Captain Vey's next responsibility was to make arrangements to have the crew transported back home. There was no British Government representative in Wilmington, so arrangements had to be made to have the British Consul come from Savannah, Alabama, to interview them, give them a living allowance, and prepare the necessary papers to get them to New York to connect with a vessel sailing to St. John's. Unfortunately, the gentleman did not provide enough money for a change of clothes. To make the trip to New York, via three buses on three 500-mile legs, they travelled in the old clothes they had on, old long rubbers and worn-out clothes. Several had their oil hats.

They arrived in New York on Friday, at six o'clock, in the middle of evening rush-hour traffic. Three taxis were waiting at the bus depot. It seemed to take forever to get to the waterfront where the SS *Rosalind* was docked. The galley was closed, so the crew went back ashore to the longshoremen's quarters for supper.

The following morning, Captain Vey had to appear at the office of the British Consul, at 15 Wall Street. He took Uncle Lew Barfitt with him, since Lew had worked in New York at one time, but that didn't help much, since he didn't know how to read. They went astray on the subway, ending up back where they started. The second time around, Wilson Vey asked directions from a fellow whose office happened to be near the consul's office, or so he thought. This was another dead end—it was two blocks away.

The two Newfoundlanders finally located the British Consul, who arranged for their passage, clothing and an allowance for food. For clothes, the consul directed them to the Seamen's Institute, filled with about 200 people looking for assistance. Vey met a fellow Newfoundlander working there, a young woman from Bonavista, who gave him a note to cover the issue of clothes. Another individual filled the order, and Vey remembers getting a pair of underwear, shoes, a sweater, an overcoat and a cap, along with a suitcase.

The *Rosalind* left New York for Halifax, and then went on to St. John's. Coming around Cape Spear, a snowstorm struck the vessel. It was Christmas Eve, and the storm dumped a foot of snow on the city. Waiting for the crew at the waterfront were the captain's sister, among relatives and friends of the crew. They stayed at Mrs. Stanford's boarding house in St. John's overnight and made it home to Long Beach, Trinity Bay the next day, December 25, Christmas Day.

Soon after the ordeal, Captain Vey wrote a letter to Sir Wilfred Grenfell, detailing the story of the shipwreck. Grenfell replied in a letter dated March 14, 1934 at London, stating that he would publish the story, and he included a cheque for $120.00.

Captain Wilson Vey continued going to sea. Several years after his ordeal aboard the *Edward VII*, he was shipwrecked again. This time he was aboard Captain Herbert John Vey's schooner, the *H. F. Wilson*, en route to Labrador, when the vessel ran into a square cliff on the Grey Islands. At the base of the two-hundred-foot cliff, everything was lost except Wilson's motorboat, in tow. The gas and oil went down with the schooner, so the crew had to row the motorboat twenty-five miles to Southern Grey Island, where the inhabitants put them up in their homes. They waited there until the mail steamer *Northern Ranger* arrived. From there, she went on to Battle Harbour before turning back to drop the crew off at Corner Brook, where they boarded the train for home.

Sources:

Daily News, December 1, 1933, p.3

Evening Telegram, November 30, 1933, p.4

Evening Telegram, December 1, 1933. p.4

Evening Telegram, December 4, 1933

Evening Telegram, December 22, 1933, p.17

Hiscock, James. Supplementary notes provided to author. February, 2000.

Kelland, Karen (Vey), and Les Vey. *"The James (Vyse) Vey Family of Long Beach."* Typescript. Second edition.

Vey, Les. *Random Reflections, Stories from Outport Newfoundland.* S. Feltham Associates Inc., 1996. p. 28-35. [From documents written by Captain Wilson Vey for Anita (Vey) Smith]

Vey, Lloyd, Roger, "Wilson Vey: Life History of a Newfoundland Seaman." Unpublished essay, 28 pages. MUN Folklore 3420, 1979

Vey, Wilson. Typescript from an original letter written upon the request of Sir Wilfred Grenfell, London. Original now lost.

Vey, Wilson. Interview, taped December 28, 1988. Captain Vey was 90 years old at the time. Recorded at Long Beach by his son-in-law James Hiscock.

The Castaway of Fish Rock

REV. JOHN ELLIS CURREY

The Castaway of Fish Rock

Hairbreadth escapes, did you say, sir? Ah, yes, I suppose we've all had more or less of them, but maybe sailors know more about them than people on the land ever can. Don't you think so, sir?" So said Solomon French, a fisherman and sealer, as he walked home with Rev. George Bond from Prayer Meeting one bright, crisp, starlit winter's night in 1889.

Rev. George Bond describes Solomon French as follows. "A good man was Solomon, a genuine, earnest and whole-souled Christian. Warm-hearted and thorough experiences had come into his life, and they had hallowed and mellowed his character, as only such experiences can."

At the Prayer Meeting just concluded, the hymns had been about the presence of God with His people in times of danger and distress. Solomon said to Rev. Bond, "As we were singin' that verse tonight, 'Oft has the sea confessed Thy power, and given me back at Thy command, it could not Lord my life devour, safe in the hollow of Thy hand,' my mind was busy enough with more'n one experience of my own in nearly forty years of knockin' about on the sea. Many a time I have seen God's hand plain enough. 'Deed I have. But when you started that verse at the close of the meetin', sir, 'Though waves and storms go o'er my head,' I fairly broke down and cried. It seemed to me that God was remindin' me once more of His great love and care for me one time, when I sung that verse in a very different place from where we were tonight. Indeed, I can never sing that verse without thinkin' of it, sir."

At this point, Solomon was going to walk on, as they had reached the parsonage gate, but Rev. Bond invited him to come in and tell the story.

"Well, sir," said Solomon, as they were seated before the fireplace, "so you've heard something of the story of the Fish Rock, eh? 'Tis a strange story, and a solemn one, too, and I can never tell it without feelin' a good deal. In the spring of 1873, I shipped out for the ice in the brig *Huntsman*, out of Bay Roberts. Captain Charles Dawe was master, and there was a crew of sixty of us, all told. We had a good ship under us, and an experienced man for skipper, a real old seal-killer. We left port on the fifth of March, and down near the strain of the Grey Islands, we were a long time doin' little, so the captain concluded to go farther north, down the Labrador coast, as the season was gettin' late, to try for some old seals.

"Off Labrador, a gale of wind sprung up, with a terrible heavy sea, and it got so rough we couldn't stand in the open water. We was forced to go into the ice for shelter, that is, sir, into a string of loose ice, three or four miles offshore. There was a couple of other crafts not far from us, and they put into the ice as well. It was now smooth, and we was far enough off from the land, bein' on the outer edge of the ice, to keep us from fearin' the lee shore, and, barrin' the danger of run-nin' into an iceberg, we was fairly safe, we thought.

"Once in the ice, we had to run with it, of course, helpless as you may say, for there was a strong tide runnin' along the shore, as well as the heavy wind and sea. Ugly enough it looked, sir, I tell ye. As night came on, and no sign of improvement—gettin' worse it was, all the time, indeed. We had some narrow escapes from icebergs as we drove along with the wind and the tide. 'Twas now several hours after dark, and we was drivin' along, every man of us anxiously watchin' out into the darkness, when we saw what looked to be an iceberg some distance ahead.

"All of a sudden, one of the crew sings out. 'Rock! Rock! On the lee bow!' The sea and the ice was breakin' over a reef of rock, dead ahead of us. Quick as thought, the skipper sung out, 'Back the headsails,' but it was no use. We drove on, right fair for the rock.

"'God have mercy on us,' says the skipper. 'We're lost! Let every man try to save himself!' 'Twas an awful time, sir, sixty of us there on the deck of that ship, drivin' right into the jaws of death, for there was no chance of escape that we could see. Four or five men jumped from the weather-bow but were smashed up at once. More took to the riggin'. With some others, I ran out onto the mainboom, but could not see any pan of ice big enough to jump onto, so I said to myself, 'I'm as well here as anywhere else.'"

Solomon French said to Rev. Bond, "Thinkin' of religion, sir, I felt thankful then for my interest in Christ, and I was as happy then as I am here in this room this minute.

"Well, sir, I was hangin' on by the toppin-lift, when she struck, bow on, against the rock, *wham*, and, as she reeled back from the blow, her stern went right under the sea and ice. I found myself rollin' over and over among the breakers that were dashin' up and over the rock. I couldn't have thought it possible for a man to live for even one minute in that poundin', grindin' sea and ice, but I did. As it dashed me

41

up on the rock, I got holt of the kelp and the stuff that was about it, and I hung on for dear life. But the sea came in and dashed me away. Again, I got holt, and again the sea carried me away.

"I got another grip, though, and I hung on, desperate, for I felt my strength givin' way, and I knew I couldn't hold out against many more seas. But again the sea dashed over me and swept me off, and I gave myself up for lost. But I managed to get holt again, a little higher up, and I said to myself, 'If another sea takes me off, I'm gone, I haven't any strength left.' I was that exhausted, I figured I was done for. Well, sir, the next sea came in to my feet and no further, and sea after sea broke on the rock and rolled that far, but not far enough to sweep me off. Then I got onto a kind of point of the rock, just big enough for me to rest my hip on the top of it and half sit, half lie, just out of reach of the sea. I didn't know if a bigger sea than usual would sweep me off. Blindin' spray was dashin' over me, constantly.

"There I was, alone on that wild rock, drenched with icy water, bruised and bleedin' from the awful beatin', holdin' on for dear life in the darkness and the storm. It was pitch dark. I could see nothin' but the white breakers as they dashed up to my feet, and I could hear nothin' but the howlin' of the wind, the roarin' of the sea and the awful groanin' and shriekin' of the ice. And yet, sir, I was kept in peace, thank God. He was near me. I could feel His hand sustainin' and helpin' me, and I sung them words that we sung tonight in the Prayer Meetin'. 'Though waves and storms go o'er my head, though strength and health and friends be gone, though joy be withered all and dead, though every comfort be withdrawn, on this my steadfast soul relies, Father, Thy mercy never dies.' You don't wonder, sir, that I can't sing those words or hear them sung without rememberin' that terrible time. Yet, blessed be God, He kept me, as I said, in peace. Oh, how glad

I was that I knew Him, that I loved Him, and that I had been tryin' to serve Him.

"It was dark indeed around me, but I had wonderful views on that rock. I could see life as I never saw it before, the value of it, the need of a man livin' wholly for God, and the awful foolishness of livin' for anything else, busy about this thing and that thing, and leavin' the most important thing of all neglected. There came to me such wonderful thoughts about God that I felt as I never had before, how poor my service to Him had been, and how different my life might be made if I had to live it over again. And, blessed be His name, I had the assurance of His love and favour, and forgiveness.

"Well, the long night wore away, and when mornin' broke, I could see somethin' of where I was. It was a dreary sight, sure enough. The ice was hove up all around me, but the wind and sea was droppin' somewhat. I could make out the hills on the mainland, four or five miles away across the ice, and not the sign of a ship or human bein', livin' or dead, in all the miles of ice around me. I was alone, famished, half dead, on that bit of a rock in the midst of the icy sea. I was so sore I felt as if I couldn't stir, and so weak I felt I had no strength to do as I wished.

"Many a time that day I sat up as well as I could and looked all around to see if I could see any sign of help or hope, but there was nothin' but miles of ice and the distant shore. It was a long day, sir, a long day. Stiff and sore as I was, it was nothin' to the pangs of hunger that began to seize me as the day wore on. That was the worst of all. It was undescribable. So I made up my mind that, as the day wore on, I'd try to crawl ashore the next mornin'. I felt I couldn't hold out much longer on the rock and that, very soon, I wouldn't have the strength to leave it. Seemed to me that God kept me from despair. I prayed to Him, hearty and often, and sung a hymn now and then to brighten myself up.

"Well, the second night passed away much like the first, except the sea had gone down, and the spray didn't dash over me at all. I could lie a bit more comfortable on the rock. But I was terrible sore and cold, and hunger was gnawin' at me more and more. When mornin' came, I saw that it was goin' to be a fine day, and that the sea was smoother than ever. I looked out and saw a great big pan of ice, so, with a prayer for God's help, I crawled off to it and started for the shore. It was slow work, sir, you may depend. I'd get over two or three pans and then take a spell, then go maybe twice the width of this room and then take another spell. I suppose in three hours or more I wasn't a mile from the rock. You see, I was beat about wonderful, and I felt my legs givin' out with weakness. However, I hobbled along.

"Then I saw three or four men comin' across the ice toward me! 'Twas a glad sight, you may depend, sir, and me heart gave big beats of thankfulness and excitement. I felt my troubles were over. They gave me a little bread and changed my old water-soaked boots, and I felt a little stronger. So, with their help, and with one more spell, I got to the land.

"But I couldn't stand when I got to their ship, and they had to hand me up. How do you suppose they came to know that I was on the rock? Well, sir, 'twas wonderful. Captain Graham, in his sealin' steamer, had been in Cape Charles harbour durin' the gale, and after it was over he went to the cape to look out over the ice with his spyglass. He, or some of his men, caught sight of somethin' movin' on the rock, and at first thought it was a seal, but then after awhile believed it to be a man. So they determined to get him off if possible. They set fire to a tar barrel to let him know that he was seen, and then the captain got about forty men to start out over the ice the next mornin'.

"So they found me, sir, as I told you. Captain Graham was wonderful kind to me, took me to his cabin and treated me as if I was his brother. I was very ill, and a mass of bruises and cuts, body and head. They brought me home on the steamer on her return, and by the time I got there I was startin' to mend fast. It was a long time before I was much good, though. I went about on two crutches all spring and part of the summer, but by the end of it I was able to walk without 'em. I feel no effects except in my feet sometimes.

"I was on the rock for thirty-eight hours. I found out that eighteen of my shipmates had been saved, but forty-one were lost. They had been drowned or beat to pieces with the ice. The ones saved had managed to get on the ice on the weather side of our ship as she sank, and they reached another ship, the *Rescue*, commanded by our captain's brother. Our captain, Robert Dawe, and his son went down with our ship.

"Now, sir, you have my story. I can never forget that time, never, never. If any man should be thankful to God, it is me. God was with me on the Fish Rock, and He is with me today. When I tell my story, and I've told it many a time in the years since, mostly to sea-farin' men like myself, I do so want to tell it, that those who hear it may see the value of faith in Christ and the power of God to keep a man's soul in peace in the greatest danger and distress. I do want to help them to seek that power if they don't possess it, and to strengthen it if they already do. There's nothin' but the religion of the Lord Jesus Christ that can keep a man straight, safe and happy, blow high or blow low, in rough water or smooth, below or aloft, afloat or ashore."

God is our refuge and strength, a very present help in trouble. Therefore, we will not fear, though the waters of the sea roar and be troubled. Psalm 46:1, 2a, 3a

But it shall turn to you for a testimony. Luke 21:13

The Faroe Island Cap

Jack Feltham

The Faroe Island Cap

Newfoundland, from the time of its discovery, has been the meeting place of people from many ethnic backgrounds. Fishermen from France, Spain, Portugal, the British Isles, the United States and Canada often found themselves toiling side by side on the Grand Banks, where all rivalry was forgotten except the drive to catch more fish than their competitors, whether they were fellow countrymen or traditional enemies.

Since bank fishermen visited the coast of Newfoundland periodically for bait and sheltered in the nearest harbour when storm threatened, there is a wealth of lore, particularly around the Avalon Peninsula, that can be traced to this source.

Bonavista Bay was remote from the centre of the bank fishery and about halfway between the routes used by ships on the way to and from the St. Lawrence basin. However, stories about vessels from this bay were not only recorded in the

St. John's local papers, but occasionally in those of Canada, the United States and Great Britain. The nine vessels from this bay that were driven out to sea in the fall of 1929 were mentioned in both the British and the American papers, mainly because one of the nine made a landfall on the west coast of Scotland, and the crews of two others were rescued by American liners. In the realm of international ocean commerce, this bay was left completely in the backwash. Sometimes in the late winter the smoke of the sealing vessels could be seen in the east. In spring, summer and fall, the coastal steamers made their periodic visits, and hundreds of schooners engaged in local trade or fishing in northern waters passed on their way north and south.

Although the north side of Bonavista Bay was remote from those parts of Newfoundland that had most interaction with foreign vessels, it was in the direct path of the Labrador current, one of the main highways of the North Atlantic. It was this natural force that brought the ice pack each spring, and thousands of icebergs each summer to the coastal waters of eastern Newfoundland. It also brought millions of seals and hundreds of polar bears to our very doorstep yearly. It was this same highway that probably brought to the north side of Bonavista Bay the Vikings towards the end of the last millennium, and their descendants, fishermen from the Faroe Islands, in 1935. Thus, the sea lore of this region is not entirely relegated to vessels of local origin.

There were other noted visitors. In the mid-eighteenth century, a French frigate was forced to shelter in Greenspond harbour in a storm. The captain later claimed that while he was harboured there, the local residents, asserting that his vessel was a wreck, robbed her of much of her supplies. In 1919, the British cruiser HMS *Cornwall* called at Greenspond and later landed a number of marines at Flat Island to squash a non-existent rebellion.

In August, 1935, the sloop *Coronet,* from the Faroe Islands, was one of the last foreign vessels to play a role in the lore of this area. This sloop was built in Grimsby, England in 1887. She was 77 feet long, 20 feet wide and 9 feet deep, with a displacement of sixty tons. Her crew were all from the Faroe Islands. With a full load of salted cod, she had set out from Greenland for her home port. The *Evening Telegram* of September 23, 1935 carried the following account of their ordeal.

> The *Coronet*, a vessel of sixty tons, with a crew of 21...On September 7 a storm came on and the vessel was badly buffeted and damaged by heavy seas. The first heavy sea broke off the foremast to the deck. Then the bowsprit was smashed off. The wheelhouse was swept overboard, taking all the nautical instruments and a little later all the boats were washed away. The vessel then drifted helplessly before the fury of the sea and without an instrument it was impossible to get a bearing...Considerable water found its way into the engine room...the men had a narrow escape from being washed overboard several times while working the pumps...Captain Jenson said that it was a miracle to him that the vessel did not run ashore in the treacherous waters off Cape Freels. The vessel had about two hundred quintals of fish on board, some of the cargo being jettisoned during the storm.

She had a 57-horsepower kerosene motor, but her fuel supply, stored in drums on the deck, was lost in the storm. The skipper decided to keep the little fuel that remained in the tank for getting his ship to shelter when and if land was sighted. He knew that the Labrador Current would eventually take them south to Newfoundland. On one of his charts there was a part of the extreme eastern seaboard of Newfoundland, which included Cape Freels and Cabot Island.

On September 20, George Knee and Harry Knee of Valleyfield were fishing about five miles southeast of Flowers Island when they sighted this vessel. When they noticed that she was without masts or rigging, they knew she was in trouble and headed in her direction. When they went alongside, they could not converse because the vessel's crew could not speak English. However, Harry Knee got on board, and the skipper indicated by signs that the motor was working and that they wished to be piloted to a harbour. The *Coronet* was directed to the pier adjacent to the Valleyfield fish plant.

There were very few outport villages along the east coast of Newfoundland where any language other than English was spoken, but fortunately in this incident there was a ready solution to the communication barrier. Mrs. Oakley from Wesleyville, while in the United States had married a Swede called Karl Anderson who was proficient in all the Scandinavian languages. They had just a little while previously moved to Wesleyville where Karl worked in a tinsmith shop owned and operated by his in-laws. In less than an hour, Anderson was on board the *Coronet* and helping her skipper make arrangements to get his vessel to St. John's.

At this time, Captain Abe Winsor owned a powered boat called the *Hero* which he used to take mail and sometimes passengers to and from Gambo. Arrangements were made through the owner's insurance company for the *Coronet* to proceed to St. John's with the *Hero* as escort. On the way south, they were delayed three days in Port Union. *The Fishermen's Advocate* of September 27, 1935, in a very brief note, mentioned the arrival of the *Coronet* at Port Union.

It is interesting to note that this vessel, fishing out of the Faroe Islands, reduced to a virtual derelict by an early autumn hurricane off the coast of Greenland, drifting for approximately fifteen hundred miles at the whims of wind and current, was given the same amount of space in this paper as that allocated to the story of a St. John's clergyman who in the same week was struck by a car but not hurt enough to be detained in the hospital overnight. It seems that the ordeal of those who wrest their living from the sea has always had little significance to editors of Newfoundland newspapers—even one called *The Fishermen's Advocate*.

Skipper Peter Blackwood from Brookfield, who was shipping his Labrador catch at the Fishermen's Trading Company at Port Union, had onboard his vessel *Willie Cave* a young man from Wesleyville called William Ford. The crew of the *Willie Cave* were constant visitors to the *Coronet* during these three days. Through the help of Karl Anderson, who acted as interpreter, Bill and one of the younger members of her crew became good friends. His name was Julius Sigmund Perkis, who came from a little fishing village called Klaksuig on one of the Faroe Islands named South West Bordo, situated about 16 miles north-northeast of Thorhavn, the capital. Before the two vessels parted the two young men exchanged gifts, and Bill became the proud possessor of a Faroe Island cap, which is still one of his prized possessions.

They corresponded periodically from the fall of 1935 until the spring of 1940. At the time Julius sent the last letter, he was an engineering student at a university in Denmark.

When the *Coronet* reached St. John's, her cargo of salt cod was sold. The vessel was bought by Captain Abe Winsor of Wesleyville, who gave her the name *Hazel Pearl* and had her schooner-rigged. She was employed in the Labrador fishery and later sold to James Tiller, who used her for the same purpose. She was lost at sea in 1946 in Trinity Bay.

The Faroe Islands, the home port of the *Coronet*, lies in the same latitude as northern Labrador, approximately three thousand miles from the shores of Newfoundland. Six years before the *Coronet* undertook this ill-fated fishing trip which made it a part of the lore of Bonavista Bay, a vessel called the *Neptune II*, owned by the Barbour family of Newtown, drove all the way across the Atlantic to northern Scotland. Perhaps the voyage of the *Coronet* can be regarded as a sequel to this event.

For eleven years, the *Coronet,* under a new name, continued to ply the coastal waters of eastern Newfoundland and Labrador until she was nearly three score years old, when she sank to the bottom of Trinity Bay. She is still remembered by some of the people of Wesleyville who sailed her, as well as others who watched her arrive and depart on her annual quest for cod. For many years she will continue to play her role in the lore of Bonavista Bay.

The Faroe Island cap will find a permanent resting place in the Wesleyville Museum, where it will be a reminder to all visitors of the very unusual visit of the *Coronet* in the fall of 1935.

William Ford, who received the cap, now lives in St. John's, Newfoundland.

The Wreck of the SS Argo

FRANK GALGAY

The Wreck of the SS Argo

The delivery of mail to and from the colony of Newfoundland was an important service in the mid-1800s. The SS *Argo* was one of a number of passenger steamships belonging to the Galway Line, officially known as the Royal Atlantic Steam Navigation Company. It was formed in 1859 by a consortium of English and Irish businessmen. The government of Newfoundland entered into a contract with the Royal Atlantic Steam Company for the conveyance of mails once a month by steam vessels plying the Atlantic Ocean in approximately six days from Galway, Ireland to Boston, and New York, via St. John's. The agent for this line was Sir Ambrose Shea of Shea and Company.

On June 28, 1859, the Galway Line mail steamer SS *Argo*, after a speedy transatlantic passage of seven days, made Cape Pine light, between 3 and 4:00 A.M. Cape Pine is located at the entrance of Trepassey Bay. Around 1850, the British

Government had built a 15-foot iron tower which contained a revolving light, approximately 314 feet above sea level.

The *Argo* was under the command of Captain Halpin, a young man twenty-six years of age, with an impeccable record as a mariner. On this voyage, the SS *Argo* carried 200 passengers, mostly in third class, which included 90 women and 30 infants, and a crew of 120 men. Halpin was fortunate to have First Officer Timothy Cummings as one of his officers. Cummings was thought to be the first native-born Newfoundlander to receive a British certificate of competence in the foreign trade, and he was known to the fishermen in Trepassey Bay and surrounding areas.

At approximately 5:00 A.M., a heavy fog settled over Trepassey Bay, a rugged coast known for jagged rocks and reefs with treacherous currents. It was commonly referred to as the Graveyard of the Atlantic because of the numerous wrecks that took place on its shores in heavy fog and stormy weather.

Despite the heavy fog which covered the area, and a suggestion from First Officer Cummings that they should reduce speed, Captain Halpin, who thought he was on course and a considerable distance from land, ordered the engine room to proceed at full speed. At approximately 5:30 A.M., the SS *Argo* almost collided with a fishing schooner which was anchored near shore. When the fishermen were asked where they were fishing, they replied, "On the eastern side of Trepassey Bay, a mile and a half or two off shore."

An eerie feeling descended on the captain and officers who were on deck at the time. The officer at the wheel gave the order "Steady" as the ship brought up to her south-southeast course. At that moment, the breakers could be seen in the distance. The engines of the SS *Argo* were stopped and reversed full speed. Before the ship got sternway, she grounded, bow-first on the rocks at Freshwater Point, eight miles from

Trepassey. Then came a sickening crash as the *Argo* hit the rocks and became stranded on the rugged coastline.

Since it was early morning, most of the passengers and off-duty crew were thrown from their berths as a result of the impact. There was utter confusion and panic on the first impact, but Captain Halpin calmed the people with the assurance they were in no immediate danger. There was an orderly evacuation from the wreck of the *Argo*, as boats were lowered away and stocked with provisions and water. The passengers left with little confusion, women and children going first. Every effort was made to free the *Argo*, as anchors passed out astern, coals were thrown overboard, and forward boilers blown off.

A reference in the newspaper *The Newfoundlander* of June 30, 1859 noted in part: "*Argo* (Galway Line) from New York gone ashore at Freshwater Point, Trepassey Bay. Agent Ambrose Shea hired steam tugs *Blue Jacket* and *Dauntless* to proceed to the scene of the wreck. Stuck on a point in dense fog, but no particulars of the unfortunate accident beyond the fact that the fishermen had complained of a current for some days previously that was strong even for that locality, so noted for shipwrecks from this cause."

Captain Halpin sent off the pilot with a Mr. Butterfield to Trepassey harbour to get assistance. When they arrived there at 10:00 A.M., they telegraphed St. John's regarding the wreck. In the meantime, provisions and luggage were sent ashore, as well as sails to make tents to protect the passengers. There was no house within eight miles of where the *Argo* struck. At approximately 5:00 P.M., the boat that left early in the morning returned from Trepassey with assurances that two boats were on the way from St. John's and that the residents were most willing and available to be of assistance. This good news quieted and comforted the passengers, who had just encountered a horrifying experience in dense fog on a hostile coastline.

There was a reference in *The Morning Post* of July 1, 1859, that fishermen in the area plundered the ship while the passengers were on board. However, in a letter to the editor of *The Newfoundlander*, signed by "A. Passenger," someone stated that he was in one of the last boats that left, and he never saw any fisherman aboard up to the time he left. The writer expressed gratitude and appreciation to the local fishermen for their concern and support.

All the passengers were landed safely, and some arrived in St. John's on Wednesday, June 29, 1859 in the *Blue Jacket*, while the remainder arrived in the *Dauntless* on Thursday, June 30.

At a meeting of the passengers of the SS *Argo* held in St. John's on Monday, July 4, 1859, Charles Miller was appointed Chairman and John H. Thompson as Secretary, at which gathering four resolutions were presented and adopted. The first read in part that "it be resolved that we deem it proper to testify publicly, to our knowledge, that before the vessel struck, the officers and crew of the *Argo* were at all times attentive, courteous and sober and appeared to do everything in their power for the safety of the passengers and ship." The second resolution referenced the agent for the Galway Line, Sir Ambrose Shea, for "his very prompt and excellent arrangements and attention in providing conveyance from the scene of the wreck," and accommodations and comforts for all of them in St. John's."

The third resolution commended the captain, officers and crew, as a body, who generally did everything for the safety of the passengers. They concluded by stating that while they were on the wreck they saw nothing wrong done by the fishermen, and that up to the evening of the twenty-eighth, the day on which they were wrecked, they treated them kindly.

Sources: *The Newfoundlander* - July, 1859
             The Morning Post - July, 1859

An Ill Wind Blows Some Good

ARDEN HALL

An Ill Wind Blows Some Good

This story of Labrador is dedicated to the inhabitants of Black Tickle. Over twenty years ago, on December 12, 1980, they rescued sixty-two Portuguese seamen when their fishing ship, the Maria Teixeira Vilharinho, *sank. A second tribute must be paid to the Canadian Coast Guard, Unit 163, based at Gander International Airport, who aided in the rescue with their Helicopter Team 301.*

The air swished and swirled like some devilish monster, and the water spewed up a venomous froth from the Labrador currents. The wind was on the land, and it was enough to make the two-storey salt-box houses creak and groan. Cool draughts of air seeped in through the single glazed windows.

May Dyson Clofield, who lived in one of these lovely houses, awoke with a start when one of the pieces of clap-

63

board siding flapped against the outer wall of her spacious bedroom. She listened to the howling winds and stared intently out between the lace curtains at the window of her sparsely furnished bedroom. Slowly, she crept back under the patchwork quilt and flannel sheets in the comfort of her snug bed. A board had fallen from the old house, and there was nothing else to see in this starless night.

May started to sink back into the anaesthetic of sleep. However, her ears picked up the vestige of another sound. It was from the outside, and then inside her home. She heard shuffling on the canvas-covered floor of the kitchen below. There was someone else astir in the house, probably awakened by the falling board. It was too loud to be her cat.

Regina Keefe McGivern, May's neighbour, knocked and called at her door. "May! May, can you hear the storm scuttling around the house?"

"Yes, maid," replied May. "It's quite a blow, enough to pull the clapboard right off the house!"

"You're right," said Regina, "and it wasn't even forecast by that cursed weather station."

May remarked wistfully, "The weather bureau is never right, and I pity anyone out on the water with this gale of wind."

"So do I," replied Regina.

Little did the two women realize that there were people awakened aboard a ship very close to their home. The seamen were commenting in the same fashion. The windy forces were increasing. Captain José Marcos and his first mate manned the bridge of a fishing trawler just off the coast, in a tickle, namely Black Tickle, where the women resided.

"The wind has picked up to fifty knots an hour," Ligouri Azaleaa, the first mate, said.

"No worry yet," replied the captain, "but we'd better stand by and not change the watch for a while. You and I can monitor the weather and await the marine forecast that the Coast Guard people send every hour."

Within fifteen minutes, the weather forecast crackled over their receiver. The prediction of a gale with driving snow from the northeast caused considerable alarm among those who heard it. José and Ligouri were apprehensive, but neither broke the eerie silence of the night. Their ship had battled stormy gales before, as did so many ships of the proud White Fleet of the Portuguese Government. Their fishing ships were now privatized, and they were more seaworthy than in the past decades, when many were wooden and prone to leaks and fires. José had been on one that sank in the Northwest Atlantic. He hadn't even gotten wet, because the ship was surrounded by other vessels. Nowadays, the steel-structured ships travelled and fished alone, and a sinking was a rarity.

Ligouri and José were in the cabin on the deck of their fishing trawler, just off Black Tickle. They were joined by a brotherly bond.

"José, it's a terrible, terrible night, with extremely high hurricane winds," said Ligouri.

"Yes, my friend. It was only supposed to be moderate northeast gales, according to the latest forecast."

"José," Ligouri said. He used the captain's first name only when the other men were not in the cabin or on deck. "It may be even worse now that we have that broken propeller."

"Ligouri, our vessel is not in her best shape right now. We should run toward Black Tickle and harbour inside. There we'll have some protection and relief from the swelling seas and winds."

"Yes, let's do that right away. The crew is getting restless. Will I tell them?"

José said, "They should be alerted and told to watch for the green light to guide us into the safety of Black Tickle. Tell them about our steering problems also."

"I'll tell the men of the danger and to watch for the lights nearby and the entrance to—"

Ligouri stopped suddenly and exclaimed, "Captain Marcos! Look! A huge wave to the starboard, and a green light between it and us!"

"Santa Maria, is it that close? I'd better run the ship slowly." Captain Marcos frowned. "It isn't responding to my wheel!"

"Oh no, it's not lit on the right anymore, and the waves are huge straight ahead."

José asked anxiously, "How far away do you think the light was, Ligouri?"

"About a thousand metres. I'll send up a flare so I can see a bit better. We don't want to be too close to the submerged rocks."

All of the crew had awakened with the knocking about of the ship. Some of them were asking, "What is happening?" They could sense that the officers in charge were not asleep or at their rest, but holding by, topside. When they saw the flare and the froth on the surface, they began to worry, and they immediately dressed with full gear and life jackets. Snowflakes were falling profusely.

Ligouri called all hands on deck. He wanted every set of eyes available to search for the beacons. One of the crew requested further clarification of their plight, and the first mate replied, "We are having difficulty with the wind, and we are steering toward shore. We must be cautious, now that we are so close to the shallow shoals."

Worried, Captain Marcos guided the boat carefully through the turbulent water, but the wind was blowing the ship off course, and the propeller shaft was so stiff and lacking in response that it was practically impossible to control. The faithful *Vilharinho*, which ran so smoothly most of the time, shuddered and broke the swells instead of riding swiftly through them. A mighty surf broke over the port side, and without warning the bottom scraped along one of the submerged reefs. The crew had seen no lights since the one that Ligouri briefly spotted earlier.

The captain yelled, "Get ready, we're on the rocks outside the tickle, and I'm going to try to swing her inside that green light ahead."

The wind had less force near the headland, and the sturdy ship swung erratically but swiftly inside the weak undertow. Something had let go on the stern of the vessel. The crew stood by the life rafts, with Ligouri reassuring everyone, including the captain, that they will make it.

The wireless operator on the ship sent a signal of SOS. A distress signal was sent and another flare fired so that anybody in the vicinity would know of the ship's plight. Around 5 A.M., the message was repeated over and over. It read ominously, "Our propeller is damaged and we are standing by the mouth of Black Tickle, Labrador. There are gale-force winds."

The crew was very silent and worried. They knew that the ship was beginning to list badly and that water was coming in through the bottom, close to the midsection where she had struck the barrier rocks. Three of the pumps were manned, but only two worked well. Some of the crew were preparing to abandon ship if and when the officers commanded it.

The first light of dawn brought the first glimmer of hope, but it faded quickly as the pumps in the back hold failed to keep up with the constant seepage. Despite their valiant efforts, the steady stream of cold, dirty sea water continued to pour in. Twenty minutes later, another of the pumps broke down as the helpless ship careened and slipped sideways, farther into the tickle. Finally, she sat firmly on the bottom in about ten fathoms of water.

Fitfully pacing, Marcos thought of the loss of the vessel, and whether her cargo could be saved for the owners. It was possible, if they obtained help before the whole vessel broke up from the constant buffeting. But his first priority was the safety of the men aboard, including himself. The people under him were of the utmost importance, more important than any shipment of cod and turbot.

The wealthy owner in Oporto, Portugal probably carried enough insurance against such a loss. Reassuring himself that this was possible, Marcos ordered the crew to man the lifeboats.

Ligouri relayed the command. He realized that this imposed another grave situation. The two boats to be lowered were on the high side of the ship, and the wind was blowing them into the vessel. *If only some rescue boats could reach them on the other side,* he thought.

Ligouri knew they had to act quickly. Despite the great risk, the two main lifeboats were lowered anyway, and lines were secured so that they didn't smash too heavily against the metal sides of the mother ship. Six of the crew were assigned to each one, and Ligouri told them to pull alongside until they were free of the *Vilharinho*. One of them got away, but the other had its lines tangled, and it smashed violently against the side, wood against metal, and the tinier craft broke up.

The crew left aboard ran to the sheltered side of the vessel and threw rubber dinghies and Mae Wests and pieces of wood overboard. Some of the more adroit and better swimmers jumped into the rough seas or fell toward anything that floated. There were lots of items bobbing in the surf. Marcos and Ligouri watched their men toss as the waves washed over them. They clung on as they drifted towards the shoreline, which was now becoming less visible in the blowing snow.

May and Regina couldn't seem to settle back to sleep. Their house was creaking and moving slightly with the force of the wind. More of the residents in the village awoke, and May and Regina decided to have a cup of tea and a biscuit before going back to their quilted beds.

At 5:35 A.M, May and Regina finished their teas and buttered biscuit. They both went to the kitchen window and looked out. There was something on the water. Instead of seeing the usual flotsam in the huge foamy surf, they spotted an orange object. As they continued looking, a bright glow materialized above the outside rocks of the harbour. It was like a fiery ball exploding and sending a shower of light down from the sky, landing close to the orange object on the surface.

"Did you see that fireball in the sky, Regina?" May asked, knowing that her friend couldn't have missed it.

"Yes, over by the headland. Someone is sending up flares and signalling. My God, look, there's a small ship coming into the point of the headland. There are figures hanging on the side of it, and others are rowing."

May was feverish. "Run to the family next door and rouse them up. I'll go to the other doors and tell them all to look out the bay. They'll know what to do. Regina, tell the Squires family to turn on their short-wave marine-band radio. There may be some news on it of what is happening."

The women made an efficient duo, and within five minutes all of the townspeople were awakened and hauling gear to the wharves to launch their boats and motorized dories. It was a sight to behold, old timers, middle-agers and teenagers, out of bed so early, racing each other to the wharves and boats.

May and Regina returned to their home and took off their housecoats and night clothes. They didn't go out again or open their windows. Instead, they cleaned away the two cups and dishes in the kitchen and instinctively prepared a large pot of soup, in case they should have visitors.

Marcos and Ligouri were elated to see that all of their crew were safely inside the boiling surge and treacherous currents, which had threatened to drag them back into the cold seas. Captain and mate were about to jump ship together when they heard their wireless: "Come in, whoever is calling SOS. We hear your signal. We are sending rescue relays to other stations. Come in. Can you reply?"

The officers hastily sent another message, which they knew would be the last before they jumped. "We are breaking up by the rocks off Black Tickle headlands. No more transmissions. Tell others of the distress and our location."

By now they didn't want to pick up any more transmissions. It was time to go. Side by side, they leaped over the rail as if they were children jumping into a pool of mud. They each gasped for breath as they hit the frigid water and bobbed to the surface, buoyed up by their life preservers. They heard a sound overhead and saw a flare shoot out from shore. One of the dories had set off an emergency flare.

The ill-fated *Maria Teixeira Vilharinho* was breaking up mercilessly. The remaining men had to be located and pulled from the cold waters to warmth and safety. José began to shiver uncontrollably in the cold water. Ligouri, who was heftier, sensed less of the water chill. He only felt the snowy ice on his face and the numbness in his lower extremities. The temperature of the water was only 35°F at this time of the year. Fortunately, it retained a little heat from the summer sun until around November, when the slob ice formed in the small bays.

The first rescuers to meet the survivors pulled the figures one by one into the boats. The sound and fury of the wind was lost to the shouts of the rescuers and loud motors of the flotilla. The first twelve seemed to be lifeless as they were lifted out and folded into the warmth of the blankets that the livyers had brought along. A few of the crew who could speak some English babbled, nearly incoherently, "The rest are still outside the tickle. Get them! Hurry!"

All those who live on the seas have a special bond, because they have experienced or known similar episodes of narrow escapes from the briny depths. Therefore, their resolve is to save all, no matter what risks they must take. As the people of Black Tickle were told of the fate of the captain and the others who were waiting outside the islands, the rescuers pushed ahead around the point to see it first-hand.

Regina finished her share of the soup-making and ran over to the Squires's house. As she entered the door, a message came over the radio. It was from a ship in the vicinity, asking assistance, and wondering if anyone else had picked up an SOS. She didn't know if anyone else had heard the messages, so she picked up the microphone and called in. "I don't know too much, except that there are lifeboats and flares outside our community."

Then another message broke in. "Hello, this is the Canadian Search and Rescue Unit out of Halifax. Can you read me?" Regina tried to answer, but before she could the operator on a vessel in the area interrupted with, "Yes, we read you on board the *Hamilton Sound*, off the coast of Labrador. We have two signals from a ship apparently sinking outside the entrance to Black Tickle." She burst in again and said excitedly over the phone, "This is Regina McGivern in Black Tickle. We have a bunch of survivors coming in to our wharves. I can see a sinking ship off our shore."

After a long pause, a message echoed over the radio. "Emergency at sea, ship in distress by Black Tickle, Labrador. Crew in the lifeboats and in the water!" There was nothing else except a lot of gobbledygook and intermittent static over the marine band, as if there were an overload. Regina left the radio and went to the stoop outside, where she beheld the rescue boats returning and carrying the strangers. Some were huddled between two local people for warmth. Captain José Marcos was one of them. He was fortunate. If he had been left in the Labrador current any longer, he would have succumbed to hypothermia. His body temperature had dropped dangerously low.

The Coast Guard's Search and Rescue Unit 163 arrived on the scene at approximately one and a half hours after daylight. Their well-equipped helicopter had travelled fast from Gander. When the crew spotted the broken vessel in the water, they noticed several smaller crafts circling nearby, like seagulls around a dead fish.

The leader called for action. He had observed the three people perched on the bridge holding steadfastly to the antennae. Captain Blackwood hovered over them. The wind from the blades was another complication, and they had to grip the antennae tighter. Blackwood's partner, Captain Vessey, opened the side door and lowered a cable and winch. Neither of the hapless trio grabbed it until Captain Blackwood shouted into an external microphone.

"Grab the cursed cable, now!"

Frantically, one of the seamen put out one hand and managed to hold it.

"Put it around something strong," Blackwood shouted.

When it was secure, Vessey lowered a harness along the cable towards the fishermen. He called over the mike for one of them to put on the harness and prepare to be hoisted up.

The bravest fellow grabbed the cable and placed the harness around his buttocks, securing it at the waist. On the signal "thumbs up," Vessey started the small motor on the winch. Slowly, the man was pulled aboard the chopper. He pulled off the harness and it was swiftly lowered to the bridge of the ship. Another seaman rose up as before. Finally, the last of the trio followed his mates.

They were whisked away to the settlement of Black Tickle in seconds. As they were flying, they spotted the local school, which had a level surface on its soccer pitch, the safest landing spot. When he touched ground, the pilot radioed in that "all was well." No one was left behind. Several townspeople walked up to the landed helicopter, their arms outstretched with a blanket for each of the shivering trio. Both flyers had big grins on their ruddy faces, a reaction to their ecstatic passengers who thanked them profusely for saving their lives. Captain Vessey just said, "It's all in a day's work, boys. Glad you're all safe and sound."

A message blared from the helicopter radio that there were two bird hunters missing around the Hawke's Bay area on the Great Northern Peninsula. Further instructions said that the rescue team was to proceed to St. Anthony in order to refuel and aid in that search. The flyers bid their new acquaintances farewell and thanked the townspeople for offering them breakfast. They insisted they must rush, that they could grab a bite while their chopper was being refuelled at St. Anthony.

May and Regina were used to ships and boats in distress. Regina had lost her husband, Norm McGivern, who was only twenty-two years old, in a winter storm several years earlier. Regina didn't speak of it at all since. Their dashed marriage and dreams were buried in the deep recesses of her soul, but she did confide somewhat to May, her friend from her school years.

May was an orphan who had inherited her parents' home when they both died of tuberculosis. The two lonely women decided to share one house in the harsh winter months to save on heating costs. Their companionship was worth the slight inconveniences of living in someone else's house every second winter. Besides, most of the time they were quite cordial with each other, and oftentimes when a tiff or difference of opinion occurred, they settled it amicably. If one were short on temper for a few days, they knew each other well enough to do something extra to boost the feelings and esteem of the other.

May, being an orphan, or chosen child of the Clofields, knew that she had a darker skin colour than her parents. When she was seven years old, they told her that she had an Innu mother called Manasee Good Shoup. They told her that her mother was sick and had died at the early age of thirty from tuberculosis. It infected her lungs and stopped her breathing. They informed May that they were not sure who her father was, but he may have been a trapper who travelled into Labrador from Quebec.

When May entered school, she was eager to learn all about the Innu in her land. She understood from her social studies teacher that Innu referred to the Montagnais and Naskaupi Indians. They were original peoples who loved to hunt and fish for a living but who also possessed small gardens and picked berries and plants of all kinds for sustenance and herbal health remedies. May knew little about the herbs, but the Clofields used Labrador tea and spruce boughs to make beer, and dandelion roots to make lots of different elixirs. Berries and bakeapples made the best wines and preserves, or jams.

She noticed some of her friends had dark skin colours, so she inquired about their ancestry. Some of her classmates told her she was not supposed to ask too many questions like that, because the older people felt that the Innu were not as good as the white settlers in the community. After all, most of the authority figures in the village were white, and they seemed to have all the answers. Even the religious leader who owned the "biggest house and church" was white. He was called the Father of all in the town. He was even the Father of the elders though he was younger in age. The elders consulted him whenever they wanted answers to expansion in their town.

May listened and watched. Even her parents sought advice from the Father or priest when they sometimes called him. They asked him about how to bring May up so that she would be an educated person and a Christian. May did what she was told and learned her Catholic doctrine, even though she didn't understand a lot of the material. For example, why was there a place called Limbo, where unbaptized Christians could not see God in Heaven? Why would a baby made by God not be able to be with God because no water of baptism was poured over its head by the priest? May liked some of the stories about the Creator better, the ones where babies and animals and flowers all were close to the Maker of the world.

Regina's ancestors were early settlers in North River, Conception Bay. They used to fish on the Labrador coast each summer, but in the 1940s they decided to settle there permanently. Her father, Jack O'Keefe, looked after the sheds and supplies for a whaling station owned by an American businessman from Mystic, Connecticut. The owner neglected his whaling chores in order to hunt and trout. He especially enjoyed catching the huge salmon and Arctic char on a fishing pole and reel. Consequently, Mr. O'Keefe pretty well ran the station for the wealthy Mr. Birdseye.

Jack O'Keefe hired many workers who were his friends in Conception Bay. They sailed to Batteau, Domino and Black Tickle in the spring when the ice broke up, and they stayed there until the fall. They caught the cod and whale and sold them to the American fish dealer. The owner, meanwhile, knew that his business was in good hands, because he made a tidy profit each and every year that Jack was foreman. Mr. Birdseye offered Regina's father a modest house and a yearly salary to oversee the plant all year, because during the winter when there was no fishing the machines and buildings needed attention.

Around October of 1940, Jack had to make a choice between enlisting in the army or going to Labrador. His fiancée helped him choose the latter, since she did not want to lose her husband. She proposed that they marry and move to Black Tickle.

In the fall of 1962, Regina's father was working one night at the fish plant. Suffering from diabetes, he had forgotten to take his insulin. Her mother sent one of her neighbours to look for him when it became very late, and the neighbour found Jack dead near one of the plant machines. He had lapsed into a fatal diabetic coma.

The neighbour ran back to the O'Keefe home and informed the family. A month or so later, Regina's grieving mother died of a broken heart. Regina was all alone and help-less and felt like giving up also. She was only seventeen, and she struggled daily to understand the tragedies in her life. Her friends gave her constant comfort and solace as she struggled to hang on to her young promising existence. Her closest friend and confidante for many years was May.

May Clofield and Regina O'Keefe shook hands warmly with the first five seamen who were brought to their door by the rescuers. The livyers thought of May and Regina first, because these two ladies were outstanding in the community for their works of mercy and common sense. They didn't have any education in organization and management, but in all of their endeavours they achieved great things. They were the captain and first mate on land, so to speak.

They gestured to the bedraggled men to enter and sit at the huge table in the warm, spacious kitchen. They immediately noticed the boiling pot of hearty soup. May gestured with her hands to her mouth and pointed to the food. She knew they were tired, cold, and hungry, so she set the hot food and rolls of bread and butter before them. The survivors glanced from the food to their hostesses, and they began to eat and drink. The warm liquid nourishment melted their stiff, aching bodies, and they began to relax. May and Regina hovered over them and watched them devour all of the soup and rolls. May knew the men were delighted with the food and that they appreciated their efforts.

The last time May had guests was for a shower for the coming of "Baby Squires," when she'd fed twelve hungry women at her lavish table. One of the women had complimented her on the fine feast, and all of the others had nodded appreciatively. This time she only aimed to fill up the hungry and weary guests. She didn't think the soup and rolls were enough, so she brought out the homemade bread and molasses. Regina produced a steaming pot of tea, and the fishermen exclaimed in delight, "Oh, beautiful food from the ladies!"

They had not eaten since suppertime on the night of the ordeal. They were famished. Two of the more outspoken older men said, "It's delicious! It's perfect! It's excellent!" May and Regina savoured the compliments as much as the men enjoyed the nourishment. The men struggled with a few English words and uttered, "Thank you, ladies." The same ritual of warm welcome would be given to the other seafarers in the other homes around the shore. All of the Portuguese fishermen would be feasted and pampered as if they were kith and kin.

The men's bellies were full, and tiredness set in. Regina called May aside and said, "They are dropping off to sleep, but we don't have enough room here."

While the men ate and talked at the table, Regina told May that the neighbours asked how they were going to manage to put them all up and feed them. The two women pondered the problem, until May thought of the largest room in the community—the gymnasium of the school.

She remarked to Regina, "We should ask Sister Jude about the school gymnasium."

Sister Jude, the principal, was a newcomer to the little village, and so far she had not involved herself in the extracurricular activities of the community. She had declined a previous invitation to the baby shower, explaining that she was too busy at the school. This certainly was true, since Sister Jude had dedicated herself to her religious teaching order. Now her mission would entail a wider involvement for which she felt inadequate and unready. When the two sweetest and ablest women in the town requested it, however, she couldn't refuse the use of the school facilities.

The remaining crew who would not jump into the ocean were snatched in slings and winched aboard the helicopter. Quickly, the Search & Rescue Squad deposited them beside the school. In less than two hours, all of the crew had been rescued from the stormy Atlantic and placed in the warm comforts of the harbour town. When the Sister Superior of the grade school gave consent to use the school, the crew sang in unison, "Thanks much, thanks."

First Mate Ligouri Azaleaa looked at Captain José Marcos and pleadingly said, "What do we do now?" It was as if he could see their future ending. In other words, now that they had no ship, where would they go from here?

Marcos replied, "Santa Maria, she will take care of us. The people here and at home will not abandon us, I'm sure, Ligouri. Don't worry so, my friend."

One of the people called upon to take care of them was the new principal, and she was unsure in her new assignment. She called all of her staff together and told them of the proposal put forth by the local ladies. The teachers immediately endorsed the plan and assured her that all she had to do was inform the superintendent of the crisis situation. With some reluctance, she called the school board superintendent in Goose Bay. When told of the grave shortage of space needed to accommodate the sixty-two new arrivals, he quickly sent a request to the Department of Education in the capital city. A message was sent back by the Deputy Minister. "Do what you feel is necessary." The superintendent assessed the seriousness of the school closure and sent a message by telephone. "Close the school, but have the staff stand by so that the students may access their books and equipment."

Sister Jude decided to follow the instructions and make the best of the temporary interruption. She advised all the staff that, despite the disruption, they should assist their students in continuing their informal lessons. The staff improvised by setting lessons revolving around the timely topics of shipwrecks, stranded seamen, and Portuguese people. The younger students got together with older students and the shipwrecked crew to research and write and draw maps of Portugal. The older students dealt with the language and culture of the people there. All began to learn a great deal of history concerning romance languages, religious piety, sea laws, economics of fishing away from home in other lands, and even marine insurance.

The owner of the *Maria Teixeira Vilharinho*, an old man named Signor Manuel Thoringa, lived in Lisbon with his married daughter since his spouse's death. He received the most shocking surprise when told that his beautiful vessel was a total loss! He was in such shock that for a few hours he forgot about the crew. His daughter reminded him that they would have to call the insurance and arrange transportation for the crew to return to their home ports. Her husband called the Lisbon insurance company, who called the major underwriter, Lloyds of London, who requested that the North American agent in Montreal investigate the claim. The local office would advance enough money on a promissory note from the owner (which would have to be reimbursed if the claim were false) in order to secure passage for each member of the ship. As long as the accident was legitimate and the report of the North American representative in agreement (that the sinking could not have been prevented), then the monies would be paid in full. Signor Thoringa would have enough to buy another vessel of similar size.

Before all of this transpired, Captain Marcos had called the consulate in St. John's, Newfoundland and requested that the consulate inform all of the families concerned. He provided a list of their telephone numbers. The people back home didn't even know that their husbands, sons, and fathers were in danger. There were numerous calls to the consulate in the ensuing days, until all of the crew had left for home.

The day after the families were notified, there was a call from Juanita Marcos, wife of José, who said in no uncertain terms, "Now that you are safe and sound, let's consider your retirement from the dangerous life at seas so distant from our native shores."

Another call came in from Signor Thoringa to Captain Marcos. "Waiting to hear what went wrong, but relieved to know that everyone was saved."

They were not only safe but as "snug as bugs in a rug," because the inhabitants had assigned blankets and gym mats to each seaman. They could rest in the cozy four-classroom school which boasted an office, a café, and a small gym that slept half the men. The other thirty-one people were split up into four groups and assigned a classroom. The men could also wash themselves there in the showers and sinks of the boys' and girls' bathrooms. The same facilities would not be available in the older homes, which were often not as warm as the insulated modern school.

Whoever thought of the idea of housing the survivors in the school deserved a pat of praise. May and Regina suggested it was mostly Sister Jude's doing. Little did Sister know that she was quickly becoming an important figure in the public affairs of the community. At May and Regina's request, Sister Jude opened the modest office, the one place she treasured as her private domain, a place where she could catch her breath and savour moments of silence during the busy school days. It had the only television and VCR in Black Tickle. She supplied the men with the several video tapes she owned. One that the crew particularly enjoyed was *The Sound of Music*.

For two days the seas were too rough for anyone to visit the site of the shipwreck, but on the third day Marcos and six members made up a salvage team. In two longliners borrowed from the settlers, they motored near the site, and two of the Portuguese men in survival suits jumped on the small part of the *Vilharinho* still showing above the surface. They forced themselves inside the top cabin and pulled out the log, a few soggy chairs, and some tobacco and cigarettes. They also found several bags floating or half-sinking under their feet, which they transferred to the longliners standing by. They passed over a couple of cases of wine. The rest would have to be salvaged by underwater crews with a lot of work, unscrewing and prising wheels and pulleys off. The agent soon to visit from Montreal would probably call the whole vessel a complete "write-off."

The occupation of the school carried over into a second week, and the staff were becoming a little impatient. However, the teachers and students learned a lot by assisting the "foreigners," and the Portuguese were happy to demonstrate their gratitude. Without doubt, the social studies and lessons for the rest of the year centred around the fishing people of Oporto and Lisbon.

By observing the older folks in the town, the youngsters learned the correct response for when such a disaster struck. They learned the often-repeated reaction, "Help each other out as much as possible."

With the shipwrecked sailors came snippets of a foreign language, and because of the relationship developed, rescued to rescuer, schoolchildren learned how to give thanks in a new way.

"Muchas gracias."

The Wreck of the Sir John Harvey

Mike McCarthy

The Wreck of the Sir John Harvey

In mid-November, 1855, the brigantine *Sir John Harvey* left the Labrador coast for her home port of Carbonear. The vessel, under the command of Captain William Penney of Carbonear, carried a full load of Labrador fish and eighty-two passengers and crew.

All went well until the afternoon of November 17, when a strong northeast gale forced Captain Penney to seek shelter in Trinity Bay. Around midafternoon the *Sir John Harvey,* still running before the gale, struck a sunken rock off Deer Harbour, just below Random Head, and began to fill with water. With pumps and buckets the passengers and crew bailed, trying to keep the ship afloat until they could reach land. Just off Green Island the ship's foreyard was blown away, which made it impossible to get the ship near shore.

At this point Captain Penney ordered the ship's anchor overboard, and the dangerous task of getting the eighty-two people on shore began. Forty-nine persons, including women with infants and small children, were landed on a rock near Green Island, where they barely had room to stand. The remaining thirty-three were landed on Green Island, some few yards distance from the rock containing the other persons.

Here the people had to stay, for their boats had been smashed in landing on the island, and even if they had saved their boats it would have been impossible to reach the shore in such weather. The storm continued to rage all Thursday night, and although their plight was known to the people in the area, they could do nothing to rescue them until the winds subsided.

It was a terrible night for the stranded persons, without food or water or shelter of any kind. Some of the survivors were lightly dressed, as they had not had time to collect their personal belongings before leaving the ship. Every effort was made to shelter the children and comfort them through that long, cold, dreary night. Three men died, one of which was Captain Penney's brother, another man Bond from Brudley who left a wife and eight children, and another young man named Norman Taylor, the only support of his widowed mother.

With the coming of dawn the wind began to subside and before long men from Little Heart's Ease and Fox Harbour came to their rescue and brought them ashore. Normally, the influx of such a large number of people would have put a severe strain on the food supply of a small community like Little Heart's Ease. However, luck was with them, for a trading schooner had taken shelter from the storm in Little Heart's Ease harbour, and Captain Penney was able to make arrangements for the survivors to be supplied with food and other necessities.

The people of Little Heart's Ease and Fox Harbour made the survivors as comfortable as they could, and after letting them rest from their terrible ordeal took them to Heart's Content on Saturday, November 19. From Heart's Content, the passengers and crew returned to their homes at Carbonear and other neighbouring communities on the north shore.

Although they had been able to save their lives, they now found themselves in a desperate condition. Their fish and all their personal belongings had gone down with the *Sir John Harvey*, leaving them without any means of getting through the approaching winter. Without a public subscription or help from the Newfoundland government, their families faced starvation.

The government came to their assistance with a grant of fifty pounds. Not to be outdone, the good citizens of Carbonear matched the government grant with a public subscription of fifty pounds. As well, the Governor and the Surveyor General each donated five pounds to the support of the survivors of the wreck of the *Sir John Harvey*.

With the help of this money, the survivors were able to make it through the winter, and when spring came, undaunted by their bad luck of the previous year, they once again made another voyage to the Labrador.

Wreck of the Camilia

Robert C. Parsons

Wreck of the Camilia

When wreckage drifted ashore at Scaterie, an island off Nova Scotia's east coast, it was easily identified as coming from the *Camilia*. However, no one in the area seemed to know much about the ship. Consensus was the debris came from a barque, but one not owned in Nova Scotia.

Scaterie Island, located off Cape Breton, Nova Scotia, lies near the route normally plied by Newfoundland coal-carrying vessels as they leave or enter Sydney. On September 9, 1891, Scaterie Island residents at Tin Cove Head discovered mute evidence of a major shipwreck: broken timbers and plank, and a lifebuoy marked CAMILIA, but more distressing, three bodies.

Since no one knew of a ship bearing that name, authorities sent a message to Halifax, which in turn relayed it to Lloyd's of London, an insurance and ships' registry office. By the next day, Lloyds replied.

"London, Great Britain, 10th Sept. 1891 It is posted here at Lloyds and sent from Halifax that three bodies, a quantity of wreckage, and a lifebuoy marked CAMILIA, ST. JOHN'S, NF, has been washed ashore at Scaterie."

From Sydney, Nova Scotia, this brief but distressing notice was sent to the P. & L. Tessier firm of St. John's, who was believed to be the owner of the vessel. "The *Camilia* is reported lost at Scaterie with all hands." So devastating was the news that the Tessier business kept it quiet for a day or so, until further confirmation. Subsequent messages confirmed the reports, and on September 11 the story broke in the St. John's newspaper *Daily Colonist* and subsequently in the *Twillingate Sun*.

The one-hundred-eighty-seven-ton barque *Camilia*, under command of Richard Harvey, left Newfoundland on June 1, 1891, bound for Brazil with a cargo of fish. She arrived safely, discharged her cargo and left Bahia, Brazil in the first week of August, headed for Sydney for coal.

From there she would deliver the coal to home port, St. John's.

According to local sources, Captain Harvey was not feeling well prior to departure and had convinced his wife to sail with him. Mrs. Harvey and one of their children made the long sea voyage from Newfoundland to Brazil to Nova Scotia. The one-hundred-eighty-seven-ton *Camilia* carried eight crew, many with large families: Captain Richard Harvey, age 30, St. John's, his wife and child; Bosun Richard Doyle, 36, St. John's, married; Cook Richard H. Rice, 29, Twillingate, married; Seaman Richard Sheehan, 35, St. John's; Seaman James Brewin, 40, St. John's; Seaman Robert Corbett, Tors Cove; Mate Arthur Colton, 33, Glasgow, Scotland, married; and Seaman John Kurgan, 29, New York, USA."

No one could satisfactorily explain what had caused the disaster. At best it could only be supposed that, upon reaching the Cape Breton shore, the barque ran into a gale and wrecked on the rocks of Scaterie Island.

It was the first major shipping loss for the Tessier brothers, who had founded their operation, P. & L. Tessier, around 1847 as a fishery-supply business in St. John's. Initially the enterprise was modest, but after 1850 the Tessiers (Peter and Lewis) became heavily involved in the salt cod trade. By the 1870s, P. & L. Tessier had become one of the largest supply and export firms in Newfoundland. In 1871 and 1873 respectively, the Tessiers exported 106,000 and 76,980 quintals of fish from St. John's, surpassing all other traders in the town.

Peter entered politics in 1864, perhaps influenced by his father-in-law, Robert Carter, of Ferryland (Peter's first wife and his second were daughters of Carter). He sat as a member of the Legislative Council while maintaining his business as a commission merchant. The firm continued for some years after Peter's death but folded in 1893, two years after the wreck of *Camilia* and the loss of ten lives.

As a footnote to this obscure tragedy, eight bodies were recovered and buried near the scene of the wreck. Nova Scotian papers published a description of those interred, and from the features described, Reverend William Lockyer, the Anglican priest of the area (who had connections with St. John's and Newfoundland) recognized and identified five. These were brought back for burial at Mount Carmel and Belvedere cemeteries, St. John's.

Saved by a Dream: Gallops of Codroy Valley

Robert C. Parsons

Saved by a Dream: Gallops of Codroy Valley

In the era of sail, deserters from the British Navy, if captured, usually suffered a swift and final punishment: hanging from a yardarm on a British ship. The Admiralty, once the most powerful naval force in the world, put much effort into finding deserters and mutineers. If those serious crimes went unpunished, the practice would become more commonplace. Often, shipboard oppression and cruelty forced men to jump ship and hide, legally making them deserters.

Just how many men who ran to escape the scourge of the British Navy and found refuge in small and isolated Newfoundland towns may never be known. But there are some local stories, maybe half truth, half legend, of founding fathers who once stood "before the mast" on His/Her Majesty's Ship.

The Gallop family originated in Newfoundland from seaman William Gallop, who swam ashore from a British man-of-war ship anchored in Lamaline. Had he been recaptured, he would have been hanged as a deserter from the British Navy, but to avoid detection he ran to Fortune, sixteen miles distant, in his wet clothes. He settled there and married Mary Kearley of Belleoram, Fortune Bay. Four of his children eventually migrated to Codroy and married there: Elizabeth (Gallop) Young, Jane (Gallop) Moore, Grace (Gallop) Martin and William Gallop.

It was at Codroy the most unusual sea experience occurred to the descendants of William Gallop. In October, 1857, Captain John Gallop's vessel *Eneman* was returning from the Labrador, when a storm capsized the boat somewhere off the West Coast. The vessel carried six crew: Captain John Gallop and his three brothers, Henry, Joshua, and Benjamin, Wilson Fiander, and a fifteen-year-old boy from England, Willie Owens, who was the cook.

Eneman carried mostly empty barrels, for the herring fishery on the Labrador that year was poor. Captain Gallop and his crew had a fair run back until they reached the mouth of the Bay of Islands. A fierce northwest gale forced them to lay to for twenty-four hours. But a high wave struck *Eneman* and she keeled over on her side, but didn't sink because of the empty barrels aboard.

Henry Gallop happened to be in the cabin and he drowned, but the others tied themselves to the rigging to survive. In the long hours facing mountainous seas and harsh October winds, they expected any moment to be their last. They were several miles offshore and had no way of getting off the wreck.

The English boy, Willie Owens, injured in the accident, died after the second day. His last words were a plea, that should any of the others survive, write his mother in England and tell her what happened.

In the long wait for death or rescue in the cold, they suffered from hunger and exposure. For three days, the will to live kept them going. Each man slept little, only to be awakened by cold wind, spray and hunger. It was in one of these moments of half sleep, half consciousness that Joshua Gallop had a vivid dream. The dream detailed how to make a boat out of canvas from the sails. Joshua convinced the others to try it. One of his brothers had a knife, so in desperation the crew decided to fashion a crude boat under Joshua's instructions.

Using canvas from the sails and wood from the bulwarks and railings lashed together with rope, they built and then-launched the frail craft. At first it sank, but they replaced the heavy keel with a lighter one and, amazingly, the makeshift cockleshell of a boat was deemed seaworthy. Using pieces of wood for oars, the survivors made the twenty miles to Chimney Cove. Four days had elapsed since *Enemen* capsized.

Chimney Cove, located between Bay of Islands and Bonne Bay, was uninhabited, but a few shacks or rough homes lined the small cove. These were used by fishermen in the spring and summer. One of the shacks contained a barrel of salted cods heads; a tiny stream assuaged their thirst, and in a garden the three survivors dug a few turnips. Three days after landing, and much strengthened, they improved their canvas boat and began the long row to Bay of Islands. On the way they met a schooner, which took them aboard and carried them to Corner Brook.

The ordeal was over. John, Joshua and Benjamin Gallop and Wilson Fiander survived a shipwreck by an amazing dream.

AUTHOR'S NOTE: Their story is recorded in *The Book of Newfoundland, Volume III*. Sometime back, many generations ago, one of the Gallops who remained on the toe of the Burin married a Forsey, an ancestor of mine.

Frank and the Beothic

EARL B. PILGRIM

Dear Frank:

As you will notice, I finally got the story finished. I have tried to make the contents of the story as clear and interesting as possible to the reader. As you read the story, there may be things in it that you may not recall, but when I went out and started asking questions and doing research in other areas, I found out things that helped me put together the story. Maybe some of the things that I wrote about you and the *Beothic* you may not recall at first—you may have been a bit bashful in telling me about it. However, I found them out anyway.

Tell your wife that I enjoyed the cup of tea, and it was a pleasure to be in your house.

To close, I hope that your family will enjoy the story. There is no doubt that there are things in it they have never heard before. If there are any questions, you can call me anytime.

Wishing you all the best, and thanks.

Earl B. Pilgrim

Frank and the Beothic

It was a calm, bright morning at Musgrave Harbour, Newfoundland on June 1, 1940. The sounds of people moving around could be heard everywhere, mixed with the loud echoes made by the dominant roosters, letting everyone know that they were kings of this slumbering town. If you listened carefully you could hear the odd cockle made by the families' hens. So it was as the young twenty-four-year-old Frank Sheppard strutted briskly along the dusty road, whistling as he went, with a few things on his mind but carefree nonetheless. Frank was spending a few days with his girlfriend Ella Hicks. He was so much in love with her that she was on his mind night and day, and for this reason he just had to come and spend a week with her.

Frank was from Indian Islands, another small town in Notre Dame Bay, a few miles north of Musgrave Harbour, and after being home for awhile following a stint at the seal hunt, he had decided to visit his girlfriend. Before he left Indian Islands, Frank had instructed the local postmistress to address his mail to Musgrave Harbour. Now he was headed down the dusty road to the post office, as he had been doing every morning for the past week.

A small man, Frank Sheppard was born on the south side of Indian Islands in the year 1916. He had spent his younger years fishing with his father, and at the age of nine he had been fishing onboard a schooner anchored under the towering cliffs of Belle Isle at the mouth of the Strait of Belle Isle. At the age of eighteen, Frank decided to leave home. In March of that year, Frank Sheppard had sailed out of St. John's harbour, heading for the icefields and the great seal hunt on board the SS *Beothic* with the renowned sealing captain Sid Hill, all flags and banners flying and horns blowing.

Excitement was at its height for this young sailor. Today, sitting comfortably in his home at Deer Lake, Newfoundland, he tells it this way. "I was young and hardy and carefree. I didn't even care if I had only half enough clothes on then. It seemed like I didn't even feel the cold. I suppose when you're young, you're tough. We would jump out on the running ice, most of the time just slob, so if you fell in, someone would pull you out and then you would go on again. The ship would go for miles before you caught up with her. To think about it now, it was awful. It's amazing that there weren't more men drowned or squat to death between the ice and the ship."

When the hunt was over Frank would come home for a few days and go on the freighting boats or go into the lumberwoods. He didn't care very much about fishing and stayed away from it.

Frank arrived at the post office and walked up to the serving wicket, noticing that the postal worker was busy sending or receiving a wireless message. This man also served the incoming mail and sent the outgoing mail by whatever means it was going. He held up his hand to Frank, indicating that he knew he was there, and Frank waited patiently until the gentleman finished his telegraph work. In about ten minutes the postman took off the headphones and came over to where Frank was standing.

"Good morning, Frank," he said with a grin. "This morning I got the letter you've been waiting for."

Frank's heart jumped. *Maybe, just maybe,* he thought.

Frank had filled in all the necessary papers to go into the navy while in St. John's. He had passed his medical and was told to go on about his normal working day. If he went home he was to make sure that he let the naval authorities know where he could be contacted. Every morning, without fail, he checked the mail.

The postman handed him the letter. It was addressed to Frank Sheppard in care of Miss Ella Hicks, Musgrave Harbour, Newfoundland. Across it was written IMPORTANT. Frank didn't look at anything else on the envelope; he saw his name and the word IMPORTANT and that was it. The postman looked at Frank as much as to say "Well, open it, Frank. I want to see what's in it, too."

The job of opening the letter would go to Ella, because Frank had promised her that when he got his letter from the navy she would be the first one to know about it. "I'm not going to open the letter until I get to where Ella is," he told the postmaster.

The gentleman understood and with a grin said, "Okay." He was thinking that if he were lucky enough to have a girl as good-looking as Ella, he would make sure that she was the first one to know everything about him, also.

Frank left the post office and headed quickly for the home of Hammond Hicks, who was Ella's father. It didn't take

Frank long to reach his girlfriend's house, his legs so light and full of energy. As he entered the door, Ella was mixing bread, with her hands full of fresh dough. She looked up as he entered, and her first glance told her that Frank had news. She could see it in his face.

"Have you been to the post office as quick as that, Frank?" she asked.

"Yes."

"You must have run, then," Ella said

"No, I walked up," he replied, "but it didn't take me long to come back."

"I'd say that you got your letter about the navy," she said, cleaning the dough from her hands.

"Yes, Ella, I got the letter," he said, as he took it out of his pocket. It was a white envelope with the address typed on it—very businesslike.

"I brought it over for you to open, Ella. I thought that you should be the first one to know about it."

Frank now wore a concerned look, and in fact, this was serious business. To enlist in the British Navy in 1940, with World War II raging, was not a small decision for a young man to make, especially with the news almost every day of people dying as ships went to the bottom from enemy torpedoes. Frank was expecting this letter to be his call. He handed the letter to Ella. Sure enough, it was a letter from the navy. She hardly knew what to say.

He said, "Ella, my dear, it doesn't matter what's on that letter. I'll still marry you."

She knew he would. They were both in love and had planned to get married in the winter. She turned around and took a knife from the countertop and quickly cut the letter open. She was uneasy, kind of scared to read it, but then as she was about to unfold the letter her mother entered the door, her hands dirty from working in the garden.

"What's going on, Frank? You look as white as a ghost," she said.

"Frank got his letter at last."

The older woman was very interested. "What does it say?"

"We haven't read it yet," said Ella.

Mrs. Hicks looked at them both, then said to her daughter, "Maybe they want him to go in the army. Last night the news said that they wanted five thousand men right away to go in the army. I heard it myself."

"I won't be going in any army," said Frank. "I'm handy enough now to the army."

Mrs. Hicks laughed. "You'll go now wherever they send you, my son. Open the letter, Ella."

"Oh, yes," said Ella as she unfolded the typed letter. "Now listen," she said. "To Mr. Frank Sheppard, Indian Islands, Newfoundland. Dear Frank."

Ella scanned the letter for a moment, then she started to laugh. "Frank, this letter is't from the war office. It's from Bowring Brothers Ltd., the same crowd that you go sealing with every spring."

"You don't mean it, Ella," said Frank, kind of relieved and starting to grin. "You almost had me in the army, Mrs. Hicks," he said, teasingly.

Mrs. Hicks was not amused. "You'll be going, Frank, my son. They got your number."

"Listen to this," said Ella.

"What does it say?" Frank asked anxiously.

"It says for you to come to St. John's as soon as possible and join the *Beothic*. Captain Penney will be in charge, and he will be sailing sometime in June, 1940."

Frank started to laugh. He put his arms around her and said, "For a moment, Ella, I thought that I was going to have to say goodbye and go in the navy."

Mrs. Hicks said, "Yes, so did I, Frank. I thought you were on your way, too."

Frank looked at her and said, "You're right about one thing, Mrs. Hicks. I'm on my way."

"Where to, Frank?" she asked.

"To St. John's to join the navy. The merchant navy!"

Mrs. Hicks could hardly talk. She loved Frank almost as much as her daughter, but now she would have to say good-bye. It would be hard to do, because Frank was such a happy-go-lucky guy. "When will you be coming back again, Frank?" she asked.

"I don't know, but I'll write Ella."

Mrs. Hicks said nothing and turned and walked back to her vegetable garden.

Frank had spent his younger years fishing with his father at what they called the trap fishery. That was not to be a career for Frank, however. At the age of eighteen, he had decided to leave home and look for something different. He had heard many tales while growing up about the great seal hunt that took place every winter and spring off the coast of Newfoundland, so when he heard on the radio that men were needed to go to the icefields, he had sent a wireless message requesting a berth. When a reply was received, he was successful. At eighteen years old, he had embarked on a new adventure; he was going to the icefields, the seal hunt, to take part in the greatest hunt in the world.

During the sealing season of 1934, Frank had been on the move. It hadn't been a very easy task to get to St. John's during the winter or early spring, of course. One would either have to walk or go on dogteam in order to get to the train at the nearest station, and in Frank's case it had been Lewisporte, Newfoundland. It had taken him close to a week to get to St. John's, walking over frozen bay ice and hitching a ride for a distance on a horse until he reached the train. In the capital city, St. John's, he had signed on with Captain Sid Hill on board the *Beothic*, Frank's first taste of the outside world, quite a difference from his quiet home at Indian Islands.

At the icefloes he had been reliable and level-headed. When not out to the seal hunt or on different ships, he was working as a woods foreman with his older brother, who was a contractor with a paper company. "I was out one spring and we got a full load," Frank said of the seal hunt. "Couldn't get another pelt aboard without sinking her. We had over forty-two thousand pelts on board. The deck was level with the water."

He was excited as he told me this, and he asked, "How much money do you think I got for my share from that load?"

I had no idea, and I asked him to tell me.

He replied, "One hundred and twenty-six dollars, and that was for the total voyage. That was cash—I had a pocketful of money!" He laughed.

At eighteen he had been a seasoned worker, and now he was a man sought after, especially for his dependability.

Ella was concerned about Frank going on the ships, because almost every day the radio news was reporting that submarines were sinking ships somewhere in the Atlantic Ocean, even close to Newfoundland. "Frank, stay home. You don't have to go on the ships. You could go to work with your brother in the woods, and that way you would be away from the submarines."

Frank just laughed it off. "Darling, I'm not going into the woods to be eaten with the flies and mosquitoes, not in the summertime."

She knew it was no use telling Frank that he shouldn't go on the ships. He was going anyway. It was what he wanted.

"I'll be aboard the *Beothic* with Uncle Charley and the rest of the boys."

"Uncle Charley and the rest of the boys won't be able to stop one of those German torpedoes if it's fired at the *Beothic*, Frank, my son."

"There's danger everywhere, Ella," he said, and he motioned to the window. "Look at your mother out there in the potato garden. I'd rather have one of those German torpedoes fired at me than get a blast from her." They both laughed.

Frank sent a wireless message to Bowring Brothers Ltd. and told them that he would be coming to St. John's on the first transportation available, preferably the coastal steamer. This done, he decided he would go home to Indian Islands for a day or so. He would have to get his work clothes and say goodbye to his parents. Ella was always on his mind, of course. Leaving her would be hard, especially now that she had agreed to marry him. He got along very well with her family. Mrs. Hicks was like a mother to him, and he knew that it would be difficult for him to leave her. That evening he secured a ride on a schooner going north, and as luck would have it, she was going to call in at Indian Islands. He kissed Ella goodbye, and leaving her with a tear-stained face, he boarded the little schooner and headed out.

When Frank arrived home, he was informed that there was a boat going to Hall's Bay. This would be the quickest way to get to St. John's; he would go to Hall's Bay, then get a ride over the Hall's Bay Line in bus and take the train to St. John's out of Badger. This is what he decided to do. The letter that he had received from Bowrings' was as good as money anywhere in Newfoundland. He only had to show the letter and some identification and it would be accepted. Frank also looked forward to getting on the train. It was always a lively time, riding in the coaches. There was guaranteed to be someone there with a musical instrument of some sort: on the old Newfie Bullet everyone who wanted to sing joined in, and Frank was no different than the rest.

Frank arrived at the Bowring Brothers complex and went directly to the marine department. He was no stranger to the personnel manager, Mr. T. Devine, who was also the company wireless operator. The manager invited him into his office and welcomed him very professionally with a hearty handshake.

He smiled. "I'm glad to see you back again, Frank."

"I'm glad to be coming back," Frank said with his gentle voice. They talked for a few minutes about the seal hunt that had taken place just a couple of months before.

"It was a great voyage," said Devine. "If we could get that every spring, everyone would have enough money." He was referring to the one hundred and twenty-six dollars Frank had made on the voyage.

Frank grinned. "You're right."

The manager pulled out a drawer labelled SAILORS. He then went through a list, alphabetically, and stopped at SHEPPARD. "Yes, right here," he said. "Frank Sheppard."

Frank was silent.

"I have your contract here, all ready for you to sign, Frank," Devine said as he handed over a sheet of paper. Frank read it over carefully.

"Is everything in order?" Devine asked.

Frank looked up and said, "Yes, sir, everything seems to be in order. But there are a couple of questions that I would like to ask, if possible."

Devine nodded and acknowledged Frank's comments. All the men were asking questions, especially now that the war was raging and Allied ships were being torpedoed every day by the enemy.

"What kind of status do we get when we go out on the ship, Mr. Devine? Are we part of the merchant navy?"

Devine took out a document from another file that read MERCHANT NAVY and then said to Frank, "This is a letter from the war office advising all merchant seamen that they are considered the same as military naval seamen, as long as the war is on and they are serving on any Newfoundland ship. It will be the same as if you were in any Royal Navy."

Frank said that he was glad to hear it "I've been to the recruiting office and filled in the papers for the navy. I did that about a month ago."

Devine looked surprised. He didn't know why Frank had not been called by now. "Well, I guess you'll sign on with us, and if you're called they'll know where to get you."

Frank nodded as he signed the contract.

"Now, Frank, there's something that we have to tell you," Devine said. "There's a cloak of secrecy surrounding all of our personnel. This is done for security reasons, and you'll be attending a briefing meeting tonight. I am instructed to tell you that you cannot tell anyone that you are assigned to the *Beothic*. You don't know who you could be talking to, you know. It could be a German spy."

"Don't worry about that," said Frank.

"I know you're trustworthy, Frank. Your uncle, Captain Charley Penney, had us contact you to sail with him."

Captain Penney had been a naval officer during World War I and had served with the British Navy. Frank's uncle had fallen in love with a girl at a young age and was planning to marry her. When the first World War broke out, Charley answered the call, joined the Royal Navy and became an officer. He faithfully wrote his sweetheart, and whenever the ship was in port, he posted a letter to her.

However, the girl of his dreams was not so faithful. She started going out with someone else and very soon fell in love with her new companion.

She continued to write Charley as if there were no other. The young girl's mother saw what was going on and asked her daughter to stop writing him, to end the lie, but she refused. It was then that her mother, for the love of one of our servicemen, wrote Charley and told him that her daughter was going steady with another man. The girl had been "putting him on," and although she pleaded with her daughter to stop, she refused. She felt so terrible, she wrote, that she decided to inform him of the deception.

As a result, Charley Penney became very bitter towards women and stayed a bachelor all his life. After the war he became a well-known captain on ships around Newfoundland and Labrador. He made his home at the Crosbie Hotel on Duckworth Street in St. John's, and this is where Frank always stayed while in the city.

Devine had someone drive Frank to the Crosbie Hotel to wait for the briefing meeting before sailing. Charley Penney was glad to see his nephew. After a firm handshake and sharing the news from home, Frank and his uncle began to talk about the war.

"It looks like a long war to me," said the captain. "The first World War was a bad one, but I think this one will be worse. For one thing, they have more modern equipment in all the forces now. You take the navy: they have guns now that can blast you out of the water ten miles away."

Frank nodded soberly. The captain went on to say, "Nothing afloat now stands a chance, especially with the German subs around. They say that the Gulf is full of them." Frank was sure that his uncle knew what he was talking about, being an ex–naval officer.

115

"Did Devine tell you anything about what we'll be doing? I mean, about the run that we'll be on?"

"No, Uncle Charley, he didn't."

"I suppose he's leaving that to Geoffrey to tell everyone at the last minute." Mr. Geoffrey Milling was the director of Bowring Brothers Ltd.

Charley continued. "The *Beothic* is chartered to the Newfoundland Railway to haul coal from North Sydney, Nova Scotia, to Lewisporte and Botwood in Newfoundland. In fact, we'll be hauling coal for the railway all year. On the return to North Sydney we'll be going to either Tommy's Arm or Roddickton to take on a load of pulpwood for Bowater's and deliver that to Corner Brook. We'll be at that job until Christmas Day or until navigation closes, which will be the end of the contract."

Frank was surprised to hear that. Usually they would be freighting around the island, carrying goods for local merchants, but this was different. He thought it might not be so bad after all. Lewisporte was not that far from Musgrave Harbour, so he might be able to see Ella on almost every trip. "That should be a pretty good run, Uncle," said Frank.

Captain Charley Penney was a very cautious man, always very watchful about his ship, no matter what vessel he was commanding. He was very good to his men. He was also a company man. If the company that he worked for wanted something done, within reason, that is if it didn't jeopardize the ship or the crew, Captain Penney would have it done, but he always put his men first.

After Frank and the captain had a lunch they headed back to the Bowrings' office. The captain went to the office that the ship captains used when they were in port. There were letters and papers waiting for him to read and sign. He then met privately with Mr. Milling about certain matters. When he came back he had a file, and in it were the papers for each man, indicating all the details about the *Beothic*—her gross tons, her rating, her port of registry. There was also a letter for each crewman, identifying them as part of the merchant navy.

That night they attended a meeting with the company officials and were given a long lecture about the war and what had to be done. They were told that security was top priority, especially the sailing dates and destinations. "We'll be sailing tomorrow morning," Captain Penney said. He took a look around. "We'll have a crew of twenty-six, including officers and sailors. Details of our destination will be discussed when we get underway. If there are any questions or concerns, we want you to ask about them now."

Several people were concerned about the war and their families. They wanted to know if there would be any changes in their regular contact with their families, regarding writing letters or sending wireless messages, or if the radio would still be giving out the boat report on the news.

Captain Penney assured them that there would be changes, especially with the radio broadcast. As far as the boats were concerned, this would not be happening. "One thing you have to remember, men, is that you are part of the merchant navy, and you will be treated just the same as if you were in the British or Canadian Navy. There's no difference." He gave each man a serious look, then continued. "Especially as far as security is concerned. And this includes everyone, that is, on the water and on the land."

Mr. Milling stepped in and assured the crew of the *Beothic* that everything would be done to ensure that security would be a top priority with the company. "If we succeed at nothing else in the coming year, we should strive for that: staying out of the way of the German subs."

After the briefing was over, Captain Penney told the crew that he wanted them all aboard by twelve, midnight, "And that will be four hours from now." He looked at his watch. "Yes, four hours from now."

Frank was surprised. He thought he would have a couple of days, or at least one night, roving St. John's. "Funny," he thought, "Uncle Charley wouldn't even tell me about our sailing time. It must be a pretty tight secret operation." However, he asked no questions.

It was just after dawn on June 9, 1940 when the *Beothic* went out through the narrows of St. John's harbour. The tug that accompanied her signalled a salute as she headed for Cape Spear and then on to North Sydney, Nova Scotia for her first load of coal. Frank said that the *Beothic* was a very gallant old girl, especially with a full load of coal, and could steam pretty well, too, if given a fair chance. She wasn't afraid of stormy weather, and the summer of 1940 was a stormy one.

"I don't know why we didn't get blasted out of the water several times, because we saw submarines on several occasions when we were coming out of the Gulf. Maybe they were friendly ones, or maybe they were German, but they wouldn't waste a torpedo on the *Beothic*. Anyway, we got away.

"There were times when Captain Penney didn't know where to go, but he kept a cool head—that was the main thing. I suppose they were after bigger ships than ours.

"We left North Sydney one time, with a full load of coal. We even had it on deck. The only thing that you could see above water were the houses. Water would come right across her. I was on the bridge, to the wheel, and I said to the captain, 'What a time for a torpedo to strike us, with this load of coal aboard!'

"Uncle Charley replied, 'You'd better know how to swim, Frank,' and then he laughed."

Frank Shepard was still concerned about that load even now, sixty-one years later.

During the summer of 1940, all was not well in the Dominion of Newfoundland and Labrador. World War II was raging in Europe and spreading fast around the world. The sightings of German submarines and the destruction caused by them around Newfoundland, especially in the shipping lanes, were of great concern to everyone. Every day the war office was calling for Newfoundlanders to volunteer to join the army, air force or the navy. In fact, the *Daily News* reported that the colony of Newfoundland was sending four times as many men and women per capita to help fight the war than the Dominion of Canada and any other country in the British Empire, outside of England herself. And this was Newfoundland's prime workforce that was leaving. Frank and the rest of the men on the *Beothic* were no different. The documents then and now say they were part of the merchant navy.

In no time, the longshoremen unloaded the coal that the *Beothic* was carrying. It would be a little more than an overnight stop. She would then head for Roddickton or Tommy's Arm and pick up a load of pulpwood, where it would take two or three days to load. Frank preferred Tommy's Arm, because he would get a better chance to see his sweetheart Ella and spend a night or two with her. This was the regular run for most of the summer and fall, and they sailed in just about any kind of weather. Only once or twice were they delayed by bad weather. Although it was rough that summer, it didn't stop her. The *Beothic* was almost always on the move. After she had discharged or taken on the load and had the proper ballast and supplies onboard she was off again. This was the way it had been ever since they had left St. John's on the ninth of June.

It was not uncommon for the small ships of the Newfoundland merchant fleet to have to run for their lives, especially whenever someone spotted a submarine or if they saw a telescope protruding from the water. Even if someone *thought* that he saw one, they all ran. At this period of time around the coastline of Newfoundland and Labrador the people lived in fear of "the Germans coming ashore one day and taking over." It was understood that everyone would automatically become slaves, that is if any survived their onslaught, and for those reasons it is thought that this is why so many young men volunteered to go and fight them. However, around the tip of the Great Northern Peninsula the fear was worse, due to the fact that it was the entrance to one of the busiest shipping lanes that helped supply the British and their Allies in fighting the war. Of course, Germany knew this and had the area included in their plan of attack. Every captain who headed towards that area was alert and uneasy. It was not a good time to be a sailor.

The great, towering lighthouse on Cape Bauld at the entrance to the Gulf of St. Lawrence was a reminder to every passing ship that its blaring foghorn and giant beaming light was not a source of entertainment or amusement. Neither was it put there as a tourist attraction. It was a guide, a beacon, and also a reminder to all mariners to be at their fullest alert while sailing in that area. It told them that the perils in the area demanded great skill from their navigators, and every captain was fully aware that to be careless in giving it the wrong code of identification or mistaking it for some other lighthouse meant a sudden trip to Davy Jones's locker.

The lightkeepers at Cape Bauld during the war years were the Fontaine family, headed by the locally famous Edward

"Ned" Fontaine, from Trois-Rivières, Quebec. They were long-serving members there. During the war years they actually sat high in the towering lighthouse and watched a naval battle take place between the German submarines and the Canadian Navy and Air Force, and then watched as the local fishermen and schooners picked up the floating debris and the spoils that covered the waters for miles around. It was said that Uncle Ned kept his cigarettes burning for seven hours, one after the other, as he watched the battle. He was ordered by the Canadian Navy to keep the light on, and he said afterwards that he didn't know if he would be blasted to bits at any minute.

Not far away, maybe just a gunshot from this giant lighthouse, was the little fishing village of L'Anse au Pigeon. It sat on a flat plateau that was nestled between two granite cliffs at the edge of the North Atlantic. This little picturesque village has a lot of history. It has been said that this is where the Vikings first landed and buried their dead around the year 1000. Some say that the great discoverer John Cabot landed here in 1497, while others say that this place was called the Isle of Demons and was the very place where the old Sieur de Roberval, "the little king of Vimeu," threw his niece and her nurse ashore, along with her lover, a young French cavalier, after witnessing an exhibition of their lovemaking. It has been said that this was around the time that the Sieur de Roberval was on his way to settle Quebec.

It makes no difference whether the colourful history of this unique little village is fact or fiction. The village was now in the hands of a salty old fishing skipper by the name of Azariah Frederick Roberts, lock, stock, and barrel, who probably gave it the most exciting period of its history and occupied it the longest. This skipper was known by many names, such as Skipper Az, Uncle Az, Uncle Fred, Daddy Wob, Grandfather and Pop. However, he was known to most as Uncle Az Roberts of the Pigeon. It is debatable whether he owned all the buildings and everything in the town, but he did own almost everything, including the Salvation Army barracks. He was not a religious man as such. He met Skipper Ned Fontaine on occasion, and it was thought that they drank heavy rum, but the Salvation Army officers who came to the town loved Uncle Az and he loved them. In fact, they all stayed at his house and ate from his table, free of charge.

When World War II broke out in 1939 and started to spread, there weren't many places on earth that didn't feel its effects, spreading fear in the hearts of people. Of course the small towns along the North Atlantic felt that they were next in line to be attacked by the Germans, due to the naval warfare that raged on the mighty oceans. The village of L'Anse au Pigeon was no different. Everyone was called upon by the war office to do his part. They could not all go overseas and take part in the fighting in Europe. They were well aware that someone had to keep the economy of Newfoundland going, and that fishing was the number-one source for revenue. However, it was made very clear to everyone by the war department that it made no difference where they were or what they were doing, they had to be involved in some way.

Az Roberts knew there was a possibility that the people of L'Anse au Pigeon would see some kind of action sooner or later, and for this reason they set out to organize themselves into some kind of defense league. Az and several other men from the area were called to a meeting in St. Anthony, a large town farther south, and they were told about the different organizations that they could get involved with. One of them was the Civil Defense League, and they eagerly agreed to have a branch set up on Quirpon Island. This was done immediately, and Az was selected as chairman. Also, a well-known businessman by the name of Esau Hillier, of Quirpon, was selected as Wreck Commissioner.

The plan was that each man would work together and organize a strong committee. They selected Gideon Hancock, Az's son-in-law, as recruiting officer for the White Bay area. They were supposed to keep their eyes open at all times, searching for the dreaded German submarines that they knew would show up sooner or later. They were organized in such a way that if they spotted anything unusual, they would relay the information to Ned Fontaine on Cape Bauld, and he would send a wireless to the war office. They were also led to believe that if the Germans came ashore, they would be using small boats launched from submarines. Therefore, as people who had never fought a war and had never even so much as seen a piece of war equipment, they didn't know what to expect. It didn't take very much to arouse their suspicion.

A story was told about an incident farther in White Bay. One night, a man went down to his stage to check on his boat, and in doing so he saw an object sticking out of the water. Right away, he started yelling, "A sub! A sub!"

In no time, everyone in the little village was awake. "What are we going to do? Should we run to the hills?" they yelled.

"No," said this brave gentleman. "I'll fix that!" He quickly ran to his house as everyone held their breath. Soon he was out with his old muzzleloader, full of powder and shot, capped and primed, ready to go. He crept like a cat, like a wild cat, down to his stage, and, holding his breath, went to the head of the wharf. There it was, right in front of him, only fifty feet away—a German submarine with her periscope up out of the water, looking right at him.

"Watch out, Hitler!" he yelled, as everyone listened in deathly silence.

BANG! went the gun. What a roar! The old gun split right in two pieces and almost killed him. The periscope was blown to bits, levelled off to the top of the water.

"I got her! I got her!" he yelled, and everyone cheered. He ran back to his house to watch further action, but all was quiet. Everyone noticed that the tide was in and the water was top high, but on the point of going out. In a couple of hours, when the water got low, a couple of the men got the nerve to go outside. They walked down to the stage and took a look around.

After a minute, one of the men came back. "I have good news for everyone," he said. "The old muzzleloader did the job all right—she blew the exhaust pipe off Uncle Henry's engine."

Several people asked him how could this be.

"Well," he said, "his boat sank to the bottom when the water was high, leaving just the exhaust sticking out, and the blast from the old muzzleloader almost blew the engine out of his boat."

One man said, "I'd say that if he was 'over there' he would sink the German Navy."

One woman who was really frightened called loudly from inside the house, "Did any of the survivors get drowned?" They all laughed.

During the summer of 1940, several sightings of submarines were made around the Cape Bauld area. One day, while Az and his crew were hauling his cod trap near the great lighthouse, a submarine surfaced not far from them. Ten or twelve sailors came out on deck and waved to the trap crew, and of course Az and his men waved back. One of Az's men held up a codfish to them. They concluded that it must have been a United States submarine, because no harm came to them. However, we may never know its identity. During this time, with all of this going on, it created a lot of worry and stress for everyone in the small village of L'Anse au Pigeon and the surrounding area. It was reported that one German sub crew came ashore one night in a place called

Degrat, less than a kilometre from L'Anse au Pigeon. They came ashore and got several barrels of fresh water.

Every evening as it got dark, the rule was that before the lights were lit the women made sure that the windows were covered with heavy dark material, to prevent any light from being seen outside. The rule was a total blackout. Also, it was a rule that all the children and even the grown-ups were not allowed out after dark. If someone wasn't home by dark, the women would say "The Germans got them for sure." It was an anxious time for everyone along the coast of Newfoundland and Labrador in the remote fishing villages.

It was Tuesday, December 3, 1940 when the *Beothic* came into the railway town of Lewisporte, Newfoundland. She was carrying, as usual, a full load of coal for the Newfoundland Railway. Shortly before coming into port that morning, they received a wireless message from the Bowater Paper Company, telling them that they were not to go to Roddickton or Tommy's Arm for pulpwood. Due to the late season and possible freeze-up, they would be prevented from loading. Everyone was happy to hear this. They received another wireless from Mr. Devine of Bowrings', telling them that they were to make one more trip to North Sydney for a load, and instead of going to Lewisporte with the load, they were to come to St. John's instead and unload there. "This will be the end of your season, wishing everyone all the best."

Everyone aboard was delighted to hear this, because it was a nerve-racking time, hearing the world news on the BBC every night and the reports of submarines being seen around Newfoundland and the Maritimes. The Germans were sinking ships almost every day, and now as the news came through that they would have only one more trip, everyone cheered.

Frank Sheppard was at the wheel on the upper deck. Captain Penney was quietly giving orders to his crew on deck as the heavily laden ship neared the dock. It took only a few minutes for the people on the dock to pull in the heavy lines and place them over the steel grumps along the front of the wharf. As the steam winches slowly pulled the heavy ship into her docking berth, Frank looked through the crowd gathered on the wharf, to see if his Ella was among them. Sometimes she would come to Lewisporte as a surprise, to spend a night with him while they were in port.

Captain Penney was standing next to him and said, "The crew have done a great job, Frank, on this trip as always. Now the job of unloading her begins." It was then that Frank saw someone among the crowd. He looked again to be sure, then said to Uncle Charley, "Look, do you see that man there among the crowd?"

Captain Penney replied, "What man are you talking about?"

Frank looked again, then pointed. "Down there in the back. It looks like Captain Stan Barbour to me."

"You're right about that, Frank, my son. It sure is Captain Stan, and he's here for no other reason than to take command of this vessel, you just watch and see."

Captain Penney was kind of shaken up, and for a minute he didn't know what to say. Frank broke the silence. "Have you heard anything about him taking over the ship, and you being relieved of your duty?"

Captain Penney looked at him and said, "Not a word. I've no idea, but I bet he's here to take over, though." He then fell silent.

The ship's walkway was put ashore, and soon people started coming aboard the ship. Frank stayed in the wheelhouse. A few minutes later, the door opened and Captain Stan Barbour came in. He wasn't all that friendly to Uncle

Charley. He quickly took a letter from his inside pocket and handed it to the captain. "This is for you, Charley—it's from Mr. Milling."

Uncle Charley took the letter and opened his mouth to thank him for it, but Captain Barbour turned and went out the door.

Uncle Charley was a quiet man who never said much to anyone, especially when it came to the running of his ship. But at that moment, Frank heard him make a nasty comment in a low voice. Uncle Charley stepped away from Frank and the two other men who were there, took out his pocketknife, opened the envelope and took out the letter. The three men watched as he read what was on it, and as he read he nodded to himself. Then he folded it, put it back in the envelope and put it in his pocket.

"Well, boys, this is the end of the line for me. Looks like I'm fired. The man that was just here will be taking over for me, and will be making the last trip to Sydney." As the men looked at him, puzzled, he continued. "I'll be leaving just as soon as I get my bags packed. In fact, I'm finished now."

Captain Penney reached up and took his cap from where it hung and put it on his head. "I wish you fellows all the luck that you can get. But let me tell you something, and I don't want to be repeated. You'll need it before this trip is over, because I would say that before the end of the trip, the *Beothic* will be on the rocks." He turned and went into his room, closing the door behind him.

Frank recalls their reaction to Captain Charley Penney's dismissal. "Well, we didn't know what to say. The three of us were in shock, but, thinking about the job that we had to do, we forgot his remarks and went and spread the word that we had a new captain."

Before the last shovelful of coal was out of the *Beothic*, Captain Stan Barbour was yelling to the crew to slip the lines.

He stood on the upper deck and told the first mate to signal the engine room to get the steam though her, meaning go ahead or astern, whatever was necessary. "Yes, sir," said the mate. It didn't take long for Captain Barbour to have the *Beothic* turned around and heading out Notre Dame Bay to the open ocean outside.

Frank was a wheelsman, and whenever the ship was on voyage he took his shift at the wheel. However, when they were in port he took his shift at whatever else needed to be done, from cleaning the kitchen sink to shovelling coal in the bunkers. He was one of three who took turns at the wheel. As they steamed along, he said to the mate, "I don't like this one little bit, Mate."

The mate looked back and said, "Why, what's wrong Frank?"

Frank was amazed that he would even ask, seeing that he had spent many years on ships around the coast of Newfoundland.

"You know the reason why," Frank said.

The mate looked at Frank as if he were mad. It looked like he thought Frank was complaining or something. "What is it, Frank, what's wrong?"

"What's wrong?" Frank nearly shouted. "Listen, can't you hear anything?"

The mate looked around, up at the ceiling, then back at Frank.

The other man who was in the wheelhouse with them quickly spoke up. "Come on, Mate, you can hear that."

The mate still looked confused.

"For goodness sake," Frank said. "The propellers are out of the water. We didn't even take on the water for ballast, and the very thing we always did before we left was take on fresh water. The pipes and everything were right by her side when we were at the dock. We're not complaining, Mate, but what we're saying to you is this. What do you think will happen to this ship when we get outside, especially if we get into rough weather? This thing will go bottom-up."

The mate started to swear. He went over to the window, put his head out through and listened to the sounds outside for a minute. When he settled back in it was obvious that he had heard the noise the propellers were making. "Did you fellows tell this to the captain before we left?" he asked angrily.

"No, we didn't, but the purser, Mr. Banfield did. I heard him talking to him," said Frank.

"And what did he say?" asked the mate.

"He told them to cast off the lines. He couldn't delay the ship for that."

The mate was furious. After he cooled down a little he said, "I don't understand why Stan would do such a thing, knowing what we could run into—especially when this tub starts to roll. Listen, boys, don't you have anything else to say about this. I'll bring this up with the captain. Maybe he has plans to go in somewhere else and get fresh water."

Nothing else was said as the *Beothic* beat her way out the bay and into the wide stormy Atlantic with full power.

The weather forecast was not good. It was calling for strong northwest gales, and the barometer was also showing stormy weather.

"Looks like a storm brewing," Frank said to the mate. "The glass is showing high winds by the looks of it."

The mate came over and looked at the glass. "Yes, it sure does, almost bottom-up." The two men exchanged worried looks, but said nothing.

About an hour after they got outside the bay, about eight or ten miles off, the mate decided to head north and go on up just outside the Horse Islands. If they struck the wind then they would have a head punch, and this way they would not be side-on to it. The ship wouldn't roll as much, and if it got too rough they could always go in under the land and anchor. They talked about this, but the mate wasn't sure. "Maybe we should call Stan up and run that by him first," he said, and Frank agreed.

The captain came up on the bridge after a few short minutes. Captain Stan Barbour was a well-known sealing captain who took many ships to the seal hunt off Newfoundland. He was known for his precise judgement in making key decisions when it came to dealing with men and ships in emergency situations. As he came into the wheelhouse he appeared to be very upset.

Captain Barbour said, "What do you want me for, Mate?"

The mate looked at Frank as if to say "You should tell him." It was obvious that Frank wasn't going to say anything, so the mate spoke. "Captain Stan, I think that we should head up towards the Horse Islands and go inside the Grey Islands."

The captain scowled at the mate and asked, "Why?"

The poor old mate hardly knew what to say. "The forecast is calling for a storm of northwest wind and the glass is bottom-up," he stammered. "Just take a look at it."

The captain didn't even bother to look at the glass. He said, "What's wrong, are you fellows frightened to death or something?"

The mate knew that it was his duty to tell the captain about the mistake that he had made. It made no difference how mad the captain got. He had to tell him how he had not taken on fresh water for ballast, and that they might as well go in somewhere and get water. "Listen, Stan, are you aware that this one got no ballast aboard her, that she sailed without taking on fresh water?"

Barbour swore. He didn't like to be told how to do his job. He looked at the map, asked the speed of the ship, then said, "If we go in around the White Bay and all around the inside of the Grey Islands, it'll take us many hours more to get around Cape Bauld, won't it?"

The mate said, "Yes, it'll take us longer for sure, but if the wind comes up northwest like it's calling for, we'll have it on the broadside all the way. And with no ballast in her this thing will be gunwaling all the time, maybe even go bottom-up."

Captain Barbour laughed. "Have you got your course set yet for Cape Bauld? It's just out from the White Islands." The mate shook his head. Barbour then took the ruler and the dividers, and in a few seconds he had the bearing. "Now steer her on this," he said, "and if you strike heavy sea let me know." He then turned and walked out of the wheelhouse as they set their new course.

They were sailing on their charted course for a couple of hours before the wind started to pick up. It quickly gathered force until it was blowing a hurricane, and drifting, just like a snowstorm. When the heavy sea started to come on, the *Beothic* started to roll, an empty ship with not a bit of ballast aboard her, and the blades out of water. There was nothing anyone could do as far as steering her was concerned, with the heavy wind on her—half the rudder was out of the water. By the time they got up as far as the Grey Islands the ship was rolling gunwale-in. All they could do was hold on in the wheelhouse.

Just before dark, Captain Barbour got kind of scared himself—he really thought she was going to roll over. By now everyone aboard knew what was going on. The ship had no ballast aboard her, and she was out of control. A huge sea rolled down, and there was no way they could get around it or away from it. They had to take it side-on. The ship rolled so much that even the air ventilators on deck went underwater, and the force of the sea was so great that they got smashed off or torn away from the deck. A lot of water went down into the engine room, and now the crew had a job on their hands to get the ventilators back in place.

The mate went into a rage. "You must be trying to drown us all, Stan! For God's sake, let her run with the sea. Haul her away, Frank!"

Now, what was Frank supposed to do? The captain was standing next to him, and Frank was a lower rank than the mate. For that reason he wouldn't alter course.

Frank looked out through the window. "Look!" he said. "There's a big one coming up there."

Captain Barbour knew what he was thinking. "Okay, Frank, haul her away," he said.

Frank turned the old *Beothic*, and she fell away and started to run with the waves. She was all right running off. They had a chance, but even running with the wind he had a job to steer her in the heavy sea, because the rudder was still partially out of the water. It took the men nearly the whole night to do the repairs on deck because they were being tossed around so much.

They were about forty miles off the Grey Islands before they ran out of the heavy sea that was kicked up by the northwest wind. They watched their chance and pulled her around head-on into it. They then slowed the engine just enough to keep up. That was Thursday night, and the wind wouldn't slack until Sunday evening. All the time they were out there riding out the storm they were iced up with the freezing spray that was going over her. The men beat off a lot of the ice, but you couldn't get it all off—that was impossible, too dangerous. The captain was afraid he'd lose someone overboard.

Saturday evening, December 7, 1940, just before the sun went down, the wind slackened. The captain ordered the men to head in towards land. It was very cool and frosty, and one of those evenings where you could see the sun hounds—the two spots on each side of the sun. Frank was on duty, and they had to get up to the upper steerage because the windows in the wheelhouse were iced up.

Frank still rubs his hands as if they were still cold when he thinks about it, although it was over sixty years ago. "I had a lot of clothes on, you know. One of those big leather coats lined with sheep's wool, and heavy rubber pants, and to tell you the truth I didn't mind it then. I suppose when you're young you're tough, or you had to be, because you didn't have another choice." Frank looks up towards the ceiling as if staring out over the ocean on that stormy night.

The *Beothic* was now heading towards land with full steam up, but they couldn't get more than seven and a half knots out of her, for the simple reason that part of the propeller was out of the water. Around ten o'clock the wind started to come around from the northeast and it came on thick with snow. Captain Barbour came up to where Frank was and stayed there. Frank noted that they could not see the length of the ship for heavy snow. By now the wind was gone, but there was a huge sea rolling. They were head-on to it, so they weren't rolling too much.

"We should have a pretty good night going up into the Gulf once we get into the Strait of Belle Isle," the captain said. He told Frank to keep his ears wide open and listen for the sound of the foghorn. "You should hear the horn on Cape Bauld, Frank. Skipper Ned Fontaine is guaranteed to be blowing that one on a night like tonight, especially with this thick snow."

Frank chatted with Captain Barbour about how rough the weather used to be when he fished with his father around Belle Isle. He said that it was funny how he could even venture out on the ocean again after what they went through. "But," he said, "I suppose a fellow forgets all about the rough times that he once had and moves on with the tide of life."

As they got closer to the land, Captain Barbour said, "I don't like it in too close to the land, Frank, because if there is a sub around, that's where they're going to be, in close to the land. Especially when the stormy weather is on." Frank was forced to agree because he didn't know anything about that stuff. These old captains, they were trained to know these things.

The snow was still thick, and they couldn't see anything. The captain said, "Did you hear anything, Frank?"

Frank said, "I thought I heard something just now, but maybe it was my mind. I've been listening pretty close ever since, but I haven't heard it."

The captain peered at him and said, "I'm going to ring down and have them slow down the engine so we can hear better. We might be able to hear the Cape Bauld horn."

Immediately after Captain Barbour rang down to the engine room, the motor slowed and so did the noise. Then they heard a horn blowing.

The captain's mood seemed to soften for the first time since the voyage started. "That's it, Frank, that's the horn that we've been waiting to hear." He put his hand to his right ear and cupped it. He said, "Listen." All was quiet, then, "Hark!" he said. "That's it, the horn on Cape Bauld, Frank, me son."

Frank agreed because the captain said so; he was the expert. He ordered that the engine again be opened up to full speed. Barbour then went down into the wheelhouse for a few minutes. When he came back, he said, "Okay, Frank. I'm going to set a course for you. From what I reckoned after hearing the horn blowing on Cape Bauld, we should be around six miles west of Belle Isle. So, with that in mind I've drawn up a course that should take us up along by the Sacred Islands and on up into the mouth of the Strait of Belle Isle. By then it should be daylight."

Az Roberts and several of his men had seen a submarine several times around the Cape Bauld area, and they had reported it to the war department. Saturday evening, there was a group of men from the Pigeon out hunting shore ducks not far from the houses, and they saw a submarine surface near the shoreline. When the men came back, Az sent some men to Cape Bauld and had the incident reported. It was a scary time, especially for the women and children, and today some of the older people in that area say that they really thought the Germans would eventually come ashore somewhere in the Quirpon Island area.

Az was very concerned with the report the duck hunters had brought back that evening. The sub had been seen a bit too close to their small town. It was like seeing an enemy tank parked on your doorstep, getting ready to fire upon you. It made them all nervous. However, life had to go on.

After the children had gone to bed, several of the men from the other houses came to Skipper Az's house for a chat and to hear the war news. Az had the only radio in the village. They were having a cup of tea around 10.00 P.M. when the question came up. "What would we do, Skipper, if the Germans did come ashore some night? What would we do?"

No one had any answers. They looked to Az for a reply. "Well, it's this way, men," he replied. "If the day or night ever comes when something like this ever happens, one thing is for sure—we won't be able to fight back. We haven't got anything to fight back with, so all we can do is try and talk to them and do the next best thing, whatever that is. We won't know that 'til it happens."

Everyone knew he was right. "Just make sure that you have your doors barred and your windows covered, where no light can get out, that's all I can say."

Staying in the house with Az Roberts and his family was the Salvation Army officer Jainey Banfield, a lovely woman.

She loved Az and his family and everyone in the little village. She was a preacher, and she also taught at the one-room school in the Pigeon. She had even married Az's grandson, Gerald Tucker, and stayed under Az's roof after they were wed. She told the people there, that no matter what happened, they were to remain calm and listen to what the Germans said, to show them kindness instead of violence. Kindness was their only weapon. After Officer Banfield spoke, the visitors went home.

The *Beothic* was in heavy seas, steaming on the course that the captain had set out for Frank. It was well past midnight, and by now the ship was blanketed with snow. There wasn't much wind blowing, but the heavy sea made it hard to keep the ship on course. The propeller and the rudder still were not completely submerged. Half the twenty-six-man crew were comfortably tucked away in bed, but the thirteen on duty were nervous, because naturally, the word had gone around that some of the crew, including the mate, were skeptical about the actions of the captain. He had ordered the ship out before taking on ballast, and their only consolation now was the talk suggesting that he may go into Corner Brook to take on ballast, now that he had learned his lesson.

At around 1:00 A.M., the captain came up on the upper bridge where Frank was at the wheel. There was heavy snow falling and very little wind blowing "How are things going, Frank?" he asked.

"You can't see very much, Captain. It's just like the dungeon. Most of the time I can't even see the head of her. I'd say that there's about a foot of snow on the deck by now, judging by what's fallen around here."

The captain glanced around. "Yes, there's a lot of snow. When daylight comes we'll get some men up here and shovel this out. Listen, you go on down and have a coffee and a sandwich. I'll take over for a spell."

Frank said, "I'll be glad to get a break for fifteen minutes or so."

He went down into the kitchen, and as he walked in he was met by young Ben Barbour, from Newtown, Bonavista Bay. Ben was the youngest man on board, and he was on kitchen duty that night. He said, "Frank, the kettle is boiling, but I don't know if you'll be able to get any water out of it or not. There are times here when it looks like the table is bottom-up. There must be an awful sea on."

Frank agreed that it was a terrible night outside, but that by daylight they should be well up into the Strait of Belle Isle and it should be smoother going up there. Ben was glad to hear that.

"I want you to make me a sandwich if you can, Ben."

"Okay. That won't be much trouble. What do you want on it?"

"Some meat, if you have any," Frank said.

"I have the meat, Frank, so your sandwich will be ready in a minute. Help yourself with the coffee if you can handle it." Ben commented on the rough trip. "It's not like the trips that we've had all year, Frank."

"'Tis blowy weather, Ben. I guess we just struck on a rough time."

Ben didn't say anything else. He knew that Frank wasn't going to say something to contradict the captain.

"Have you heard the war news tonight, Ben?" asked Frank.

"Yes," he replied, "they had a full hour on. It started about nine o'clock. There was an awful lot of people killed over there in a battle somewhere. I just forget the name of the place."

"My son, we haven't seen the end of this war yet," Frank said gravely. "I'd say that the Germans will be over here to take over Newfoundland yet."

"I wonder what they're like hauling cod traps?" Ben said with a laugh.

Frank knew that this eighteen-year-old kid didn't care about anything. Fear wasn't in his vocabulary.

When Frank finished his lunch he quickly moved back to the upper deck and took the wheel from Captain Barbour.

"I think I'm going to stay here on the bridge 'til daylight, Frank," said the captain. To Frank he seemed a little nervous. The captain then asked, "Were you talking to Tom Bursey on your way up?" Tom Bursey was the other man on duty with Frank. He was in the lower wheelhouse and was also watching the compass and the direction that Frank was steering, just to make sure that he didn't go off course. One acted as a check on the other.

"Yes," Frank replied.

"Did he tell you how fast we're going?"

"Yes, we're doing eight and a half knots."

Captain Barbour shook his head. "That's not very fast."

Frank didn't answer. It was around 2:00 A.M. on Sunday morning.

Frank Sheppard gets tears in his eyes every time he tells the story of the last few minutes of the *Beothic*. She was a gallant ship that served her masters well, but if she had been treated fairly she would never have gone down on that frightful morning, December 8, 1940. All was going well on board as she twisted and turned, creaking as ships do in heavy seas.

The captain said, "Frank, what time have you got?"

Frank looked at his watch and said, "I can't see. Just a minute." He flicked his lighter and took a look at his pocket-watch. He remembers saying, "'Tis twenty-five after two."

"Well, in about four and a half hours it should be daylight, and it might clear off," Captain Barbour said.

Suddenly, Frank looked straight ahead. He thought he saw something. He blinked his eyes, then looked again. "Captain Barbour," he said quickly, "that looks like land to me, straight ahead!"

Captain Barbour almost jumped out of his skin. "Where?" he yelled.

"Right ahead, 'tis land!"

"My God!" the captain cried. "Frank, you're right!" He jumped from where he was standing to the controls that led to the engine room, and he grabbed them and pulled them down to full astern, but Frank felt a heavy thump, like a sudden drag, like something had grabbed onto the ship's bottom. She immediately slowed in.

"Then she struck," recalls Frank. "The stem head hit smack into the cliff and she came to a full stop, the same as if she had hit a concrete wall. It's a wonder that the captain and I didn't go right over the bridge. If we had, we would have dropped about thirty feet onto the steel deck, and you know what that would have meant—sudden death."

Down in the engine room there were six men who shovelled coal—they were called stokers—and the two engineers. They were having their two-o'clock lunch break, just sitting to the table when the bells rang to reverse the engines to full speed astern. The engineer said later that he didn't even get a chance to get to the throttle before she struck.

"The men in the engine room told us that they thought another ship had rammed them or that they had been hit by a torpedo. They never dreamed that they were ashore. As they were running to get out of the engine room, they saw the bottom split right open, but they all got out.

"As we were huddled low for a few seconds on the upper wheelhouse deck, kind of peeping over the rail at the very cliffs around us, a huge wave rolled in. It literally lifted us up, the whole ship, and slammed us side-on into the cliff. Well, to tell you the truth, I thought we were all gone. For a moment I couldn't see any hope."

Barbour roared, "Frank, let's get down out of this into the wheelhouse!" The two men didn't take the stairs, but jumped down the eight feet and went inside to where Tom Bursey was. Tom was holding onto the wheel for dear life with his eyes wide open.

"We're ashore!" Frank said to Tom.

Captain Barbour made a loud roar to the wireless operator, a Mr. Spurrell of Wesleyville, Newfoundland, but before he got a reply, young Ben Barbour came through the door. He still had his cook's apron on. "What's happening, Captain?" he yelled. "Are we torpedoed?" No one answered. Then the eight men from the engine room came into the wheelhouse, wearing nothing but shirts and overalls.

The captain told the assembled crowd what they already knew. "The ship is finished—" He stopped as a heavy wave came and threw the *Beothic* farther into the cliff.

"—abandon ship and go to the lifeboats!" He turned and said, "Frank, take charge of getting the lifeboats overboard. We'll need at least three to take everybody."

They went outside to where two of the lifeboats were, noticing that the stern of the ship was already below water. As they started to launch one of the lifeboats, the rest of the men arrived. A couple of them had heavy coats on, but most of them had been in their bunks mere seconds before. Some of them were wearing just sweatshirts and pants, with nothing on their hands or their heads, and the snow was as thick as mud. Frank split the crew into three groups and had each group go to a lifeboat. They worked on launching three boats at once.

The captain came out and said, "Frank, get a head count. Including me there should be twenty-six. The purser and the wireless operator are in the wheelhouse with me—we're trying to get a message off, an SOS message—so there should be twenty-three of you out there. And make sure that everyone has a life jacket."

The first lifeboat to get off was manned by Abe Bragg of Pouch Cove. Abe was just as tough as a dog. He didn't care if he was in the water or out. There were times when the sea came right over him, but he just held on and told the rest of the fellows with him to do the same, and of course they did. It was good to have excellent men in key places at a time like this. There were seven of them; they had the lifeboat all ready for when the sea came in, and when it did Abe gave the signal and she went off clear of the ship, just like the squid, with seven men on board. They all knew what to do. The four oars went overboard at the one time. Abe was smart: before he went, he tied a rope to the ship, so that when he got away, he would have a line back to the ship, because once you got clear of the ship you couldn't get close to her again to fasten one, for fear of getting swamped.

Carman Noseworthy of St. John's was in charge of another lifeboat. He was an older man, but he knew what to do. They were about to put that one out the same way when the crew on the other side started yelling to Carm. Frank ran over to where they were. It was the mate. He said, "Listen, Frank, we can't get the lifeboat off on this side because the ship is close to the cliffs. She has to go out on the outside like the other two."

The mate was right. Frank recalls, "I yelled out to Carm to come over with his crowd and help launch it across the ship. The men ran over and almost picked it up and carried it to the other side. Men become twice as strong, you know, in a time like that."

When Frank looked around, he saw Abe Bragg getting a rope near him. "How did you get here, Abe?" Frank asked.

"I came back hand over hand on the rope from our lifeboat to the ship." He had dragged himself through the water and back to the ship to give them a hand!

Captain Barbour was pushing the wireless operator to get an SOS out. Finally, he got in contact with one of the coastal steamers that was tied to a wharf in St. John's harbour. They took his message. In the meantime the crew were all saying to the captain, "Look, Captain, you better come on now, because we could go bottom-up any minute!" But Captain Barbour wouldn't leave until he got the message out.

"The sea was heavy and the ship was thumping wildly," Frank remembers. "But she was tight, up against the cliffs. The two lifeboats were off in fairly safe water, or at least out clear of the breakers. We got the lifeboat that we had to go in around to the other side. We put the captain in the head of her and he had hold of the rope that was going out to the other lifeboat. We told him that when the sea was right we would give her a push and everyone would jump aboard, and he was to haul on the rope to get her clear before the sea ran out. Abe was roaring from outside to us, telling us to get ready. He roared, 'Come on!' and with that we gave the push, the captain hauled on the rope, and off she went. Well, we jumped aboard. As we did we heard the men calling out from the two lifeboats.

"It only took about half a minute and we were out clear of the ship and the breakers, but the mate and the purser were still aboard the ship. It was a job to see them due to the snow that was falling and the darkness. We had five flashlights, and although it was dark, it was one of those nights when you could see fairly well. Now we had to deal with the fact that there were still two men aboard and no lifeboat aboard for them to get in, not even a rope back to her.

"Abe called out, 'We'll take them off.'

"The three lifeboats then got together, and Barbour asked Abe what his plan was. 'Listen, let your two boats string out ahead of us. That'll be one, two, three tied together. When the sea calms down a bit, ease us back and I'll throw a line to the boys aboard the ship, then I'll go aboard with another line, and that's the one that we'll haul them out with. I'll make sure that they're tied on good. This is the only way.'

"The captain okayed it. He had no choice. In about half an hour, we had them all off the ship. Then in the darkness we looked at her. She was gone down by the stern, all of her back houses were underwater. The water was almost up to the upper deck, but the head was up out of it. We knew that it would be only a matter of a few heavy swells and she would be gone under. As we looked at her, we thought about all our suitcases and heavy clothes and everything else that we had left aboard. Some fellows had their summer's pay, or what was left of it, in their trunks or suitcases. I didn't have any money in my trunk—I was lucky that I had given it to Ella on the trip before—but I had all my clothes, that is dress clothes, left behind. I lost that and my personal stuff, you know, the little things that you gather."

They were all off the ship and on board the three lifeboats, that was the main thing. Captain Barbour was in a very sorrowful state. He could hardly talk. He knew that he was going to have to answer a lot of questions, especially about why he left the wharf in Lewisporte without taking on ballast, and for not going up along Canada Bay closer to land where it was smooth, like the mate wanted. Instead, they had ended up forty-five miles outside the Grey Islands where the seas were as mountains.

There they were, at 4.30 A.M., wondering which way to go. As they moved off a ways they recovered their senses and started to talk among themselves. The captain figured they had hit the back of Belle Isle, gauging the distance between here and back where they had heard the foghorn at the Cape Bauld lighthouse. No one knew for sure. "The only thing that we can do now is go off, clear the land and wait for daylight," said the captain.

Everyone but Frank was in agreement. "Listen, boys," he said. "This is not the back of Belle Isle. I fished on the back of Belle Isle for years, and I never saw any place like this out there."

"Well, where do you think we are, Frank?" said the captain.

"I'm not sure, but we should go off, clear the noise of the sea and listen for the sound of a foghorn. For sure on a night like this they'll all be blowing."

Barbour agreed and told the men to start rowing off land. By this time they noticed that the snow was starting to ease up. There were seven or eight of the men who had next to nothing on—only short-sleeve shirts and light pants—as they had jumped out of bed with haste. They were cold and shivering, so the captain made them row to keep their blood flowing. Frank had a lot of clothes on, so he took off his inside shirt and gave it to young Ben Barbour; he was just a young man, and all he had on was a T-shirt and, of course, his apron. He was one of the men who were made to row in order to keep warm. Of course, everyone had life jackets on, the ones with the slabs of cork in them. That helped a little.

They tied the three lifeboats together and got down low in them. It would have been preferable if they'd had a piece of canvas or something to go over some of the fellows who were wet. Anyway, shivering and tired and dispirited as they were, a foghorn started to blow. Everyone said "Listen" at the same time. The sound was coming from the northeast.

"I still say that sound is coming from the lighthouse on the eastern end of Belle Isle," said the captain.

Almost everyone agreed. Frank didn't say anything, but Hubert Banfield, the purser, spoke up. "What we should do now is start rowing toward that sound. At least we know there's something out that way."

The captain ordered the men to start rowing towards the sound. The *Beothic* crew rowed for about an hour. It had stopped snowing completely, and the stars began to appear. Up ahead the men saw a high mountain they didn't recognize. All they knew was that it was somewhere around the tip of the Northern Peninsula.

"I think it's starting to get daylight," someone said. They could see a little light in the eastern sky.

"The sooner the better," said the captain.

In less than half an hour daylight was starting to break upon them, and when it did they finally realized where they were: about half a mile off Degrat.

It was a tradition around all the small fishing towns that whenever you went to bed—it made no difference whether it was early or late—the fire was put out first. People were afraid of fire. There were no furnaces in any of the houses, and no one had oil stoves burning all night long. No matter how cold it got, it was unheard of in the outports of Newfoundland around this time. Saturday night, after the crowd left Az Roberts's house, the fire was put out and all the lamps extinguished. Az took all the heavy material down from the windows, so that during the night they would be able to see any light out on the ocean.

Az had a man under his roof by the name of Norman Pilgrim who was his son-in-law, married to his oldest daughter, Winnie. Just as daylight broke on this clearing Sunday morning, Norman got up and came downstairs to light the fire, and Carl, aged seven, the eldest of his three children, trotted downstairs behind him. Before going to bed, Carl had spotted a large, hot fruitcake that had just come out of the the oven, and he knew that when he came downstairs with his father he was guaranteed to get a slice. As Norman was lighting the fire, Carl jumped up on the couch and looked out through the window. Although there was a little frost on it, he could see the outside fairly well.

Carl is very clear about the incident and remembers it quite well. "I got up on the couch while Dad was lighting the fire, because the floor canvas was so cold. There was no doubt that I was going to get a piece of that big cake that was on the table. When I looked out through the window, I thought that I caught a glimpse of something coming in the harbour. I looked again, then, sure enough, there they were: the Germans, as far as I was concerned. I said 'Daddy, Daddy, the Germans are coming in the harbour!'

"'Okay,' he said, without even looking up. I said again, 'Daddy, there's boatloads of men coming in the harbour!'

"Dad looked at me as I jumped down from the couch. He stood up and looked out. 'My God!' he roared. 'They're here, Carl!'"

Az Roberts and his wife, Emily Jane, had their bedroom off the kitchen and their bedroom door was never locked, but on that morning a lock would not have stopped Norman. He burst into the room, screaming, "They're here, Skipper! The Germans are here, they're coming in the harbour in boats!"

Az got out of bed in an awful hurry—in fact, in one leap.

Carl said to Az, "Granddaddy, the war is coming ashore."

Az went to the window, and sure enough, there they were: three boats, side by side, full of men heading into the Pigeon. "Get everyone out of bed!" Az said as he dashed back into the bedroom to get his clothes on. As he was hauling on his pants, he told Norman to tell Jainey the Salvation Army officer to put on her uniform quickly.

In five minutes, Jainey was in the kitchen, dressed in her uniform, ready to go. Az pulled on his skin boots and his winter coat, then said, "Get me the Union Jack." This was the official flag of the Dominion of Newfoundland. Az had one that was on a six-foot pole. As he was going through the door, he said, "Don't anyone come out of doors."

Norman said to him, "Shall I get the guns ready, Skipper?"

"No," Az replied, "look after the crowd." He then took the Union Jack and stuck it up over his shoulder. With the Salvation Army officer walking near his side, they headed down to the wharf, ready to conquer the Germans with kindness.

Augustus Bridger, known as Uncle Gus, was also lighting his fire on this early Sunday morning. He looked out through the window and saw the three boats coming in the harbour, and he too thought that the occupants were definitely the German navy, so he said afterwards. However, Uncle Gus was not like Az. He went for his old muzzleloader. He poured in the powder and shot, put in the wad and punched it solid tight into her.

Uncle Gus crept down to his stage without anyone seeing him and went out to the front. He lifted up a small hatch near the splitting table, and sure enough, there they were: boatloads of men, all armed and ready to fight, as far as Uncle Gus was concerned. He said to himself as he leaned his elbows on the splitting table and levelled the muzzleloader at the men in one of the lifeboats, "I'll wait first 'til they go to tackle Az and the Army officer, then I'll at least kill what's in one of the boats."

Az and Jainey walked out to the head of the wharf. Two men got up out of the lifeboat, and Az knew at first glance that they were not navy men. They were all covered in coal dust and smeared with black oil. He knew that this was a shipwreck crew.

147

"My dear men," he said, "who in the name of God are you? Are you Newfoundlanders?"

"Yes, I'm Captain Stan Barbour."

"Stan!" said Az. "What in the world?" They knew each other from way back. Az could hardly believe it. "Were you torpedoed?"

"No," said Barbour, "we went ashore."

"Jainey!" cried a voice from one of the lifeboats. Jainey thought she recognized the voice, but she couldn't focus on who it was. The man came up out of the boat and ran to her. "Jainey, my blessed God, it's you! Jainey!"

For a moment she was dumbfounded. Finally, she blurted out, "Hubert!" It was her brother Hubert Banfield, the purser. It was the first time they had seen each other for over two years.

When Uncle Gus saw one of the men get up out of the boat and put his arms around the Salvation Army officer, and one of the men shaking hands with Az, he lowered his large gun, took the cap off her and walked out on the wharf. Everyone looked across at him. Az said later that Gus looked like an old pirate, ready to tackle the enemy.

"This was one morning of my life that I will never forget," said Frank Sheppard. "I knew Az Roberts. I had been in L'Anse au Pigeon before and had been to his house, and now here I was again on his doorstep, part of a shipwreck crew, cold, wet and frightened. But for us it was all over. We were about to put our feet in under Uncle Az Robert's table—we knew that we would be taken care of. To us it was the same as if we had gone to heaven. We were in an awful state; you know what it's like aboard one of those coal burners, and especially aboard the *Beothic* that was carrying coal all that year. You could hardly touch a thing aboard her without getting into a state, and when the sea started to wash over her, I bet everything was turned black for miles around. Well, that Army officer had a job to recognize her own brother.

"The whole lot of us walked into Az Robert's kitchen that Sunday morning. I'll never forget it. Now, mind you, there was an awful mess that came off us—you could slip around on the floor with the grease—but Aunt Emily Jane, Uncle Az's wife, and the other women there didn't mind that. Their biggest concern was to get the wet clothes off us and get us something to eat and a wash. We moved down into the cookhouse that Az had for his men during the summer fishing season. Now, Uncle Az used to have a big crowd of men summertime, so this is where we stayed for the next two days."

After the men had dried their clothes, found something else to put on and had something to eat, they pulled up the three lifeboats. Then they went and launched one of Az's trap boats. The captain wrote a message, and Uncle Az sent a man along with two of the crew to Cape Bauld, to send a wireless to Bowrings'. The message read as follows: "*Beothic* struck in a heavy snowstorm near Cape Bauld. Crew safe. Expect a total loss. Signed Captain Stanley Barbour."

Az sent a couple of men to Quirpon to get the word to Esau Hillier, the Wreck Commissioner for the area, so he could take the necessary action of notifying the government and the public of the fate of the *Beothic* and the crew.

Frank went in the boat along with Uncle Az and Norman Pilgrim, and of course Captain Barbour and the chief engineer. They went along the shore looking for the ship. They didn't know for sure where she was, so they went along by Rangalley Head and crossed the area out from Little Quirpon. Then, just as they went around the point outside that area, they saw her. She was broadside to the cliffs. Her head was up out of the water, as well as part of her forward hatch and all of the wheelhouse and the smokestack. It looked awful.

They went in alongside her. They thought that they were going to get aboard her, but there was too much sea on.

"It's too risky to go handy to her, Stan," said Uncle Az. "We should go on to Griquet and notify Fred Bussey at St. Lunaire. He might get a crowd together and come down to see if they can salvage some of your stuff." Frank and the others were glad to hear that.

They went on to Griquet and got the postmaster to go in the office and send a wireless for them. It read, "To Mr. Geoffrey Milling, Director of Bowring Brothers Ltd., St. John's, Nfld. Sir: Regret, *Beothic* a total loss. Ship broadside to cliff, stern submerged and engine room flooded. Position about two miles east of Griquet. All crew safe." This message was released to the *Daily News* on Monday, December 9, 1940.

Another message was received by Mr. T. Devine of Bowring Brothers Ltd. from Mr. Esau Hillier, Wreck Commissioner, Griquet, Nfld. "*Beothic* a total wreck, stern underwater, engine room flooded, no possible chance to refloat her, captain and chief engineer here. Her position about two miles from Griquet. All crew safe."

In the late afternoon they went back to the wrecked ship but couldn't get handy to her. They returned to L'Anse au Pigeon, where the men stayed for the next two days. On the third day they received a wireless telegram instructing them to proceed to Griquet and wait for the coastal steamer the *Prospero*, which was on her way from Corner Brook and would pick them up in a few days.

"We all went to Griquet in the afternoon and were welcomed with open arms," said Frank. "The people took us in. It was all free, you know. They fed us, gave us clothes and treated us just like your mother would treat you. In fact, in the night they held a dance, a square dance, and what a time we had!

"What caught my eye the most was that all of the women that were out in the dance had skin boots on. Yes, they were out in the square dance, cracking it right down, with skin boots on. My son, 'twas something to see." Frank is eighty-four years of age, yet he remembers as if it were yesterday being twenty-four at the town of Griquet in the year 1940.

One of the boys found out why Captain Barbour had been in such a hurry to get out of Lewisporte and on his way, and why he wouldn't go up close to Canada Bay. He told Uncle Az Roberts that the night before he took over the *Beothic* he had received word that there was a submarine seen around Englee, and he was afraid that it was waiting for them to go up to Roddickton to get a load of pulpwood for Bowaters. So he had kept way outside, and it had cost him dearly. It had cost him his ship.

The crew of the *Beothic* spent another four days at Griquet before they were picked up by the coastal steamer *Prospero*, and from there they went to the town of Little Bay Islands. Frank was discharged on December 18, 1940, as per his service papers. He worked as a foreman in the logging industry for many years, and later he became a carpenter, until he retired. Since then, he has been a volunteer for different organizations, including the Red Cross.

• • •

Frank took down a large picture of the *Beothic* and handed it to me. "There she is, Earl," he said. I noticed that the picture had been taken when she was out to the icefields at the seal hunt. Frank pointed out the large toilets built of wood that were out over the back end of the ship. "There used to be around two hundred and twenty-four sealers on board when we were out to the ice, and this toilet was a very busy

151

place—especially just after the cook served the men a feed of fresh seal meat!"

Frank laughed. He pointed to a couple of large packages that were hoisted up and strapped to the rigging. "What do you think that is up there, Earl?"

I looked closer, then said, "I don't know. You'll have to tell me."

He laughed and said, "That is two quarters of fresh beef. There were no freezers on board, so the cooks kept the fresh meat hung up in the riggin'."

"I guess that kept it cool and fresh," I said, and Frank laughed.

Three Pilots Lost off the Narrows

ROSALIND (WAREHAM) POWER

Three Pilots Lost off the Narrows

On Friday, November 29, 1929, the Norwegian freighter SS *Hertia* was in trouble about 35 miles off St. John's. She had run out of coal and was burning the woodwork to keep going when the American freighter SS *Saguache* took her in tow and headed for St. John's. Twice the tow lines parted, and the ships made little headway in the terrible gale which had sprung up Friday night. But by Sunday afternoon, December 1, the lights of the steamers were sighted off the St. John's Narrows.

The crew of No. 1 Pilot Boat at King's Wharf, near the eastern end of the harbour, prepared to go out to the incoming ships to guide them in safely, a job they had performed many times before in all kinds of weather. By 6:00 P.M., the pilot boat was steaming out through the Narrows past Fort Amherst Lighthouse, with four pilots on board: Pilots Lewis, Walsh, Noseworthy, and Vallis, the latter in charge of the motor. Pilot Lewis had nearly missed the boat, as he had been at home suffering from a cold when he was telephoned. He reached the pilot station just as the men were going down the hill to the boat.

The pilot boat, belonging to the St. John's Pilotage, was an old, waterlogged trap skiff, built years earlier by Vokey's in Trinity Bay. It housed an Acadia 2-cylinder, 20-horse-power engine in a domed engine house which was high enough to allow a man to walk around inside. It was not equipped with flotation tanks and could easily sink if struck or overturned. It was not the safest craft to be plying the waters of St. John's Bay.

As the pilot boat slipped past the north and south heads of the Narrows and turned toward Cape Spear, the two ships were seen to be moving away. At that time the weather was not particularly stormy, so the pilots decided to wait out by Cape Spear and see what the ships were going to do. When the ships turned in the direction of the Narrows again, the pilot boat went toward them to board a pilot. A wind storm had been brewing since Friday, and the lull they were now experiencing would not last for long. Each man was probably well aware that the open roadstead of St. John's Bay offered no protection from any wind, which could whip the waters into a frenzy in a minute. It was a risky place to be on a dark winter's night, and each man was probably deep in thought as they motored toward the ships.

Among the four men on board the pilot boat there was a surplus of skill and experience. Captain George Ernest Vallis and Captain Levi Samuel Noseworthy were deep-sea captains who had commanded foreign-going sailing ships for many years. Captain Vallis's first command, the *Horatio*, had been sunk by a German submarine off Portugal during World War I. Another of his vessels, the *Margaret Swartz*, was lost at Mistaken Point near Cape St. Mary's, Newfoundland, with no loss of life. Another vessel under the command of Captain Vallis, the *Annie L. Warren*, was sunk behind the *Kyle* in Harbour Grace, Conception Bay, Newfoundland. He was the first master of the beautiful *Edith M. Cavell*, which was sold to the Portuguese fishing merchants who copied her lines for their famous White Fleet.

Captain Noseworthy also had his share of adventures. He was in the tern schooner *Ruth Hickman* when she was lost off the Irish coast and was picked up by a British warship. There was no loss of life in that shipwreck, however Noseworthy broke his leg leaping from the vessel to a lifeboat. In October, 1924, his schooner *Freedom* sank at sea in a terrible gale. When he abandoned ship, Captain Noseworthy decided to run for Barbados, 600 miles away! It was an epic journey in two small boats, but everyone made land safely, including his two young sons, aged eight and ten. A few years later, Captain Noseworthy left the ocean routes and joined the local pilot service. Perhaps Noseworthy, like Vallis, decided to leave the unpredictable deep-sea life when the steamships started to replace the sailing ships, or maybe both men opted for a less dangerous job near home.

Captain Vallis, age 40, hailed from Coomb's Cove, Fortune Bay. He had joined the pilot service three years earlier, in June of 1926, when a vacancy opened up due to the death of Pilot James Brown. Noseworthy, age 50, was also new to the service, having joined just one year earlier, in September, 1928. He took over the position of Captain S. C. Duder, who had been appointed as St. John's harbour Master. Both Vallis and Noseworthy had worked for the A. S. Rendell Company and lived near each other (Vallis on Sudbury Street and Noseworthy on Hamilton Avenue), so it is likely that they were friends before they entered the pilotage service.

Next in seniority was John Walsh, age 59, who was in the service twelve years, having joined in November, 1917. Walsh came from one of the oldest families in the East End of the city, and in his early years was a crack oarsman at the St. John's Regatta. He was well-known and liked along the waterfront, easily making friends and always ready to do a good deed. When he was a young boy he had gone to work at Baine Johnston's Southside premises. He entered the pilot service at age 47, training under Master Pilot William Vinicombe before he earned his pilot's licence.

Eliol Broomfield Lewis, age 60, was practically born into the pilot service, having come from a long line of harbour pilots. He was an apprentice pilot in July, 1895, and in August, 1896 he stood in for his father, Charles Lewis, when the latter became ill. A year later, at the age of 28, he was granted a pilot's certificate and joined the crew of No. 2 Pilot Boat, with William Lewis, Frederick Lewis, and Apprentice George Lewis, his brother. The Lewis name had been associated with piloting since the early 1800s, when the pilotage service consisted of four boats, each owned by a master pilot and manned by his relatives.

Most likely Eliol Lewis was trained by his father and had started as a "mullinger." A mullinger was a man hired on to row the pilot boats back in the days before engines. Each pilot boat hired on several men to row the boats, and the most promising was kept on and trained to be a pilot. When the man earned his pilot's papers and started earning his pay, he was required to turn over half his earnings to the man who had trained him, and then the old pilot retired. That system ended when it was challenged by a pilot who didn't want to give his money away.

The 1921 census stated that Walsh and Lewis lived on Signal Hill Road and were both born in St. John's. They were only one year apart in age, so it is likely that they were long-time friends, having lived close to each other before working together for at least twelve years. With thirty-two years of experience, Eliol Lewis was the senior man in the pilot boat. Walsh was second in line, while Noseworthy and Vallis were the junior men.

As they neared the two ships, they lined up the pilot boat with the SS *Saguache* first, and Pilot Lewis climbed up the ladder and boarded the ship. Although this was a routine feat, it was fraught with danger. On January 31, 1898, Pilot Lewis had nearly lost his life when his foot slipped on the ladder as he was disembarking from the SS *Barcelona*, and he was hurled into the water. Fortunately, the ship's captain was watching and reversed engines, or Lewis would have been chopped to death by the propeller blades. He was hooked out by his fellow pilots and rushed to shore. This time, however, the passage from boat to ship was made without incident, and Lewis headed for the bridge to take over command of the vessel to bring her into port.

Meanwhile, the remaining three men in the pilot boat tied onto the ship and hitched a ride, which wasn't an uncommon thing to do when so far from the entrance. Lewis talked with the men in the pilot boat several times, and they said they were riding all right, as the ship was barely under steerageway. They proceeded that way for 30-45 minutes until it began to get stormy again, and the men asked the *Saguache* to "come to" so as to make smooth water for them to shove off. They were either heading for the *Hertia* to board Pilot Walsh, or they were heading for the harbour.

It was then that something went terribly wrong. The pilot boat apparently capsized, for someone on the *Hertia* heard a shout and saw a man struggling in the water alongside the ship. When the *Hertia* reported to the *Saguache* that they feared something had happened to the pilot boat, the ship

159

halted its forward progress and came about to search for the men. It was now about nine o'clock and pitch black, with a heavy sea building in the northeast gale, and freezing hard.

A wireless message was sent to shore, requesting the service of a tug to assist in the search. As soon as Marine & Fisheries received the information, arrangements were made for the tugs *Hugh D* and *Moulton* to go to the rescue. It was about 10:00 P.M. when they got underway from the Furness Withy Wharf, with Captain Stan Duder, the Harbour Master, accompanying the search party. After searching the area of the accident for three hours and not finding anything, they assumed that the pilot boat must have sunk immediately, taking the three pilots with it. The search party returned to port at 1:00 A.M.

Meanwhile, the two ships with Pilot Lewis on board had put out to sea again, as it was now too stormy to attempt an entry.

The next morning, at eleven o'clock, the Marine & Fisheries Department announced the tragedy to the *Evening Telegram* and notified the families of the victims.

Three widows and fourteen children were left to mourn the deaths. Captain Vallis's wife Bertha sent to school for her children to come home. When young Claude walked in the door, his mother was sitting by the stove. She turned around and with tears in her eyes said, "Poor Daddy is gone."

Young Wilson Lewis, nephew of Eliol Lewis, was delivering papers that morning when one of his customers said that three pilots had drowned last night. Wilson ran all the way from Water Street up Barter's Hill to Pennywell Road. He ran into his house and told his mother, who collapsed with shock into a chair.

News of the terrible tragedy quickly spread around the city as relatives, friends and neighbours rallied round to comfort and support the widows and children of the lost men.

Eliol Lewis finally got the two ships into port on December 4. He had been under considerable strain with the responsibility of the vessels for two days and two nights in stormy weather, coupled with the shock of the loss of his comrades. He was very distressed when he reached port and broke down when questioned about the accident.

For a couple of days rumours were flying around the city: i.e., someone had seen the pilot boat in Cuckhold's Cove; the boat had been found bottom-up; several sailors had drowned trying to save the men, etc. There was also much speculation about what had actually happened to the pilots. Questions were raised about why the boats had gone off so far on such a stormy night. Many forgot that when the pilots were going out that night there was a lull in the storm, which helped in their decision to go out as far as Cape Spear.

Nobody knew for sure what had happened, as no crew members on either ship actually saw the accident. It was felt that the pilot boat overturned after it left the side of the *Saguache*. Perhaps it was swamped by the seas. Others felt that the boat may have become fouled in the tow rope between the two ships and overturned. The boat would have sunk quickly, as it was not equipped with flotation tanks. Some crew members thought they had heard a man scream and saw someone struggling in the water, holding onto an oar. Perhaps he was the pilot who would have been shoving off the boat from the side of the ship. The other two men may have been trapped in the engine house when the boat sank.

The *Saguache* and *Hertia* left St. John's on December 7, 1929. Many people voiced the opinion that they should not have been allowed to depart until an inquiry was held, as those on board both ships were the only witnesses. When questioned about the accident, both captains stated that they knew nothing. It was felt that if one ship was towing the other, then there must have been a watch at the bow on one and at the stern of the other. Either man on duty would have been aware of the position of the pilot boat, and if questioned might have thrown some light as to what had happened.

The questions remained. Was the pilot boat overturned by the tow rope? Was it crushed by one of the ships? Was the accident preventable? It was felt that an inquiry would answer such questions. However, there was no inquiry, and the drowning of the three pilots was deemed an accident and nobody was blamed. The three vacant pilot positions were filled by J. Legge, A. Benson, and George Anstey. Captain George Anstey became guardian of Captain Vallis's children.

A week after the accident, Captain Duder set up a relief fund for the children of Captains Noseworthy and Vallis. People were very generous, even though pocketbooks must have been stretched to the limit. At that time, people were collecting for the tidal wave victims on the Burin Peninsula, Christmas funds for several orphanages, the Salvation Army, the Christian Brothers, plus the victims of ten missing schooners which had gotten caught in the same storm as the *Hertia* and *Saguache*. By December 17, $2,281.60 had been collected. Mrs. E. R. Burgess also donated three tons of coal. Captains Noseworthy and Vallis were members of the Masonic Society, who paid for the education of the younger children.

There was meagre coverage of the pilot tragedy in the local newspapers. Perhaps this was due to the great tidal wave disaster just two weeks earlier, which occupied the news every day. The latest reference to the drownings came from New York.

A letter dated December 11, 1929, addressed to the pilots of St. John's and from the New York pilots, stated:

Dear Sirs. I am enclosing a clipping from *The Boston Herald* of last week. I wish to express my deep sympathy to the families of those who were lost in Pilot Boat No. 1. The different American newspapers all spoke highly of your courageous exploit. Wishing you Christmas Greeting, I am, most sincerely, Joseph Sullivan.

United New York Sandy Hook,
Pilots' Benevolent Association,
New York

After December, the pilot accident ceased to be an item in the local papers. There were never any bodies or wreckage found, and the drowning and disappearance of three harbour pilots on December 1, 1929 became another mystery of the seas.

Captain Levi Samuel Noseworthy, age 51, left wife Barbara, age 43, two daughters, Lillian, age 23, and May, age 21, two sons, Gerald, age 15, and Robert Samuel, age 14.

Captain George Ernest Vallis, age 40, left wife Bertha, age 41, six children, Queen, age 19, Etta, age 17, Robena, age 15, Claude, age 13, Jack, age 9, and Hazel, age 7.

John Walsh left wife Bridget, age 46, and three daughters, Mrs. Mary Furlong, age 29, Mrs. J. P. Murphy, and Gladys, age 26, who was away in Boston when her father drowned. He also left an adopted son, James, age 9, and a stepdaughter, Bride, age 25.

Eliol Lewis remained in the pilotage service until July 31, 1941. He was then 69 years old. He died two years later, on May 14, 1943. He had been in the pilotage service forty-six years.

EDITOR'S NOTE: The writer, Rosalind (Wareham) Power is a granddaughter of Captain George Ernest Vallis. Her mother was Etta Vallis, aged 17 at the time of her father's death.

The Stranding of the SS Kristianiafjord

CAPTAIN JOSEPH PRIM

The Stranding of the SS Kristianiafjord

Thousands of vessels have been stranded and wrecked around the coast of Newfoundland and Labrador, but none caused more concern than the grounding of passenger liners. Some of those transatlantic vessels which operated around the turn of the twentieth century were little bigger than our present-day coastal vessels. However, this was not the case of the Norwegian American Liner SS *Kristianiafjord*, owned and registered in Norway, and was 10,670 gross tons, 530 feet overall, with a cruising speed of 15.5 knots. She carried 100 first-class, 250 second-class, and 850 third-class passengers. Built at Birkenhead in 1913, this was the first vessel built by her owners who named her for Norway's capital city Kristiania, now Oslo.

The *Kristianiafjord* left New York on July 7 for overseas ports via Halifax, from which port she departed the thirteenth of July. On board were 900 passengers, 250 of a crew. Her

167

freight consisted of dairy products, various meats and cheese, also a large quantity of sugar consigned as a relief shipment to the wartorn country of Belgium (she was always known in Newfoundland as the "Belgium relief ship"). Other cargo carried at the time included 1,500 tons of copper ingots and bar lead.

Having departed Halifax, a course would be set to pass off Cape Race about five to ten miles. From there a great circle route would be followed to the English Channel. After passing the island of St. Pierre and Miquelon, her track would be running almost parallel to the eastern section of the Newfoundland south coast, across the mouth of some of the largest bays on the island, Fortune Bay, Placentia Bay, St. Mary's Bay and Trepassey Bay. When water floods into those bays, twice every 24 hours, millions of tons of water are flowing in, dragging unsuspecting vessels navigating in restricted visibility farther onto the land. When the tides are ebbing, the opposite effect occurs.

As a mariner, I have experienced such an occurrence many times when sailing past this section of coast. After departing Halifax for St. John's, a course would be set to pass five miles off Cape Race. On occasion, if the base course was not corrected by a change in a compass heading, the vessel might arrive at a position fifteen to twenty miles off Cape Race. At other times, with no apparent effect from wind and sea, a position in the area of Cape St. Mary's was arrived at. Such a drift was not caused by compass error, as a Gyro compass was used, which has very little error compared to a standard magnetic compass.

No doubt a set to the north caused the grounding of the SS *Kristianiafjord*, on July 15, 1917, in restricted visibility. All that night she had been running at a reduced speed as required by the International Rules of the Road. This action no doubt gave her more time to set in on the land.

At the time of her loss, a vessel had no means of determining her geographic position in restricted visibility. One year after the loss of this vessel, a radio direction-finder (RDF) was installed one mile west of Cape Race light by the Canadian Government. Such direction-finding equipment gave the vessel a bearing, and helped to determine her position, although never truly reliable, but a big improvement, and eventually became a requirement on all vessels.

The stranding occurred at 4:00 A.M. in Bob's Cove, which is located about seven miles west of Cape Race. A distress signal was immediately transmitted by wireless and received by Cape Race and by other vessels in the area. The Canadian vessels SS *Stanley* and *Sable Island*, which were en route to St. John's, offered to take on board 153 persons and departed for St. John's. During this operation, other passengers were being landed on shore.

Bob's Cove is a small dent in the coast exposed to wind and sea from east to west, the shoreline is devoid of vegetation from the high-water mark to 70-80 feet up a sixty-degree angle, and then continues for another 50 feet to the top. From a shale- and boulder-covered shore the top is covered by rolling hills, sod and marshland for miles, very little scrub, but a few stunted trees—one of the better places to run ashore in a smooth sea.

Cape Race had notified St. John's of the stranding, and immediate rescue plans were put in place. A coastal vessel and tug were dispatched to the scene and a train was also sent to the closest rail station, Broad Cove, by 9:00 P.M. The train had taken on board 626 survivors and at ten o'clock departed for St. John's.

A press release from St. John's stated, "St. John's NF. Norwegian steamer *Kristianiafjord* ashore 7 miles west of Cape Race, master reports landing passengers and requesting assistance, Canadian steamer *Stanley* standing by, sending steamers *Portia* and *Petrel*.

After the arrival of the tug, efforts were made to tow the vessel off the rocks, without success. Larger salvage tugs were requested from Halifax. The captain was optimistic that his vessel could be refloated with the aid of compressed air supplied from the larger tug. However, this method of refloating a grounded vessel had never been developed. When a salvage tug arrived from Halifax and divers made a survey of the bottom, another press release was made.

"Kristiania, Norway, July 21. According to a telegram from Captain Hjortadahi dated Cape Race, July, divers have examined the bottom of the steamer *Kristianiafjord* and found the vessel is resting on an even bottom and not straining much. Some damage was found under No. 2 and 4 holds, but the engine room and stokehold and the rest of the hull is apparently undamaged."

On the same date several salvage vessels were alongside the casualty, and one already loaded with salvage cargo had arrived St. John's. The following release was made:

"St. John's, NF. July 21. With much of the cargo removed, the prospects of refloating the stranded liner *Kristianiafjord* near Mistaken Point under existing favourable sea conditions are bright. The divers have closed the holes, thus greatly facilitating the work of refloating the ship. No water has gained access to the engine room or cabins. The work of salvaging the cargo goes on apace and is being carried out by schooners and small steamers. Stevedore T. Godden with 20 experienced men have gone out yesterday and is looking after the landing arrangements, and already two schooners and the steamer *Tremble* have arrived here with cargoes of salvaged goods while the *Ranger* is due this afternoon with another load and two cars of luggage by the Trepassey train today."

Meanwhile, at St. John's every effort was being made to accommodate and feed the stranded passengers. Various charitable service organizations were requested to help, and they responded in the usual manner. Women and children were housed at the Seamen's Institute, first-class passengers were given quarters on board the *Florizel*, men were quartered at the Prince's Rink, Grenfell Hall, and British Hall. Most personal items were salvaged from the wreck and brought to St. John's by the SS *Prospero* and tug *Petrel*, and over 2,000 suitcases and trunks were landed at Shea's and Crosbie's premises, where survivors lined up to claim their personal belongings.

Many important people were travelling on the *Kristianiafjord*, which was a neutral flag vessel, as Norway was a neutral country during the First World War. Its vessels could travel the oceans of the world without being harassed by German U-boats.

Another release from St. John's dated July 29 stated, "A furious storm last night made a hopeless wreck of the Norwegian steamer *Kristianiafjord* which ran aground two weeks ago. The work to lighten the cargo was in progress, and with good weather it had been hoped to float the vessel this week, but she pounded heavily in the sea raised by the storm. The crew, numbering 250, who remained on board were forced to abandon her. She was going fast to pieces when the last of the men left her. The crew will be brought to St. John's tomorrow."

Arrangements were made by *Kristianiafjord's* owners to have the Swedish American vessel SS *Stockholm*, which was in Halifax at the time, to proceed to St. John's for the survivors. This was carried out by August 5. They were embarked and on their way to Gothenburg. Before leaving they thanked the government for the expedient way in which they handled matters, also the people of St. John's and the Southern Shore for the kind treatment given since their ship went on the rocks.

The final news release from the wreck dated St. John's August 13 stated, "The wreck of the steamer *Kristianiafjord*, which stranded at Mistaken Point and became a total loss, was sold by public auction as it now lies on the rocks and was bought by Hon. M. P. Cashin for $2,600.

We can only speculate as to the actual cause of the stranding of this new vessel, which no doubt was fitted with the latest navigation aids offered at that time. The most practical explanation would be that she was set on the land by a flood tide running in the bays. Operating at a reduced speed also gave her more time to set to the north.

Compass error was blamed by some people, which was very unlikely on foreign-going ships. They are checked and cross-checked at sea on a continuous basis. The amount of metal carried in the cargo was also blamed for attracting the compass. This theory was disproven, as the metal carried was non-ferrous and would not interfere with a magnetic compass. Under the circumstances, the only navigation at the master's disposal was a sounding lead. This was of little value when running parallel to the coast.

This was not the first passenger liner to run ashore in this area, and not the last. It makes one wonder why a course was set to pass so close to Cape Race in restricted visibility while on a European voyage, when there is a thousand miles of ocean on the outside.

The First Time Andy Short was Shipwrecked

SHANNON RYAN

The First Person as a Narrator
"The First Time Andy Short was Shipwrecked"

During the 1970s I carried out a series of interviews with retired fishermen and sealers in Conception Bay, Newfoundland. Mr. Andrew Short (1900-1989) was one of my chief informants. The following personal experience narrative is part of an article, "The Personal Experience Narrator as Historian: The First Time Andy Short was Shipwrecked," published in the *Newfoundland Quarterly* (Vol. LXXIII, No.2, Summer, 1977).

Andrew Short, born in Kingston, Conception Bay, first went to the Labrador Coast as a young child with his father who fished at the White Bear Islands. As he grew up he fished with his father and brother Sam, and later in partnership with Sam. Like other Labrador fishermen of his generation, he worked as a miner at Bell Island, Buchans, and North Sydney, and he went sealing regularly. (He was on board the *Ungava* in 1933 when Captain Peter Carter brought in the heaviest cargo of seal pelts ever landed in St. John's, and on board the *Beothic* in 1934 when Captain Abram Kean brought in his millionth seal.) On occasion he also sought employment as a sailor, and it was in this occupation that he experienced his first shipwreck. (His later shipwreck experiences occurred while travelling to and from the Labrador coast.)

In 1946, Mr. Short moved his family to Riverhead, Harbour Grace. For some time he continued to fish on the Labrador coast, but later he found work in Goose Bay and Sept-Îles (then Seven Islands). In the early 1950s he began fishing out of Harbour Grace, selling his fish fresh to the fish plant owned by the family of Frank Moores. He retired from fishing for health reasons in the mid-1960s.

Politically, Mr. Short supported the Liberal Party until Frank Moores entered politics in 1968. Because of their long-term relationship, he switched his support to Mr. Moores and campaigned for him. Up until his death he campaigned for the Progressive Conservatives, first Frank Moores and Haig Young, and later for Morrissey Johnson, Brian Peckford and others. He remained active in many areas until near the end of his life. For example, in 1985, at the age of 85 he was chosen by Morrissey Johnson (Federal) and Haig Young (Provincial) to direct the installation of an artesian well and waterline on Fishermen's Road, Riverhead, where he lived. This line, now connected to the Harbour Grace water supply, is still in operation.

Uncle Andy was a natural-born storyteller, as one can see from the following story about his first shipwreck, and I am sure he would be proud to have his story published in this collection.

Shannon Ryan

The First Time
Andy Short was Shipwrecked

The first time I was shipwrecked I was twenty-four. That was the first spring I was to the ice.[1] We came home from Labrador; my father, he was skipper of the vessel.[2] When we went up to Brigus to moor up the vessel[3], the *Vendetta*, this vessel was over to the government wharf. So I went over aboard her, looking around. At that time it wouldn't be many three-masters[4] we used to see, and I was interested in that stuff.

The captain was on deck, Captain Sam Noseworthy. I didn't know him, just the same.[5] He said he was short of hands, couldn't get a crew.

I said, "Captain, what about a berth?"[6] This was about the twenty-eighth of October. She was going to Sydney[7] for a load of coal; she was in the coal run, see.

He said yes. He told me the story. All hands was after leaving her, cook and all. She was an old vessel, and they didn't like her. She was a hard vessel to work on because there was no hoisting engine[8] on her, and she was one of those big heavy vessels, a very hard vessel to work.

So he asked me if I could get a few more for him for a crew. So I said I'd try.

So I got Tom Power in Carbonear[9], and I got Jack Hearn from Carbonear, and Fred Rossiter. Fred Rossiter was only about sixteen years of age at that time. The train was running on the North Shore then.[10]

When I went home I told me father. He said, "Boy, look, if you got any luck on your side, leave that old thing alone, because if that was any good you wouldn't get any berth on her. She wouldn't be hung up now two weeks looking for a crew to go to Sydney." She was about three hundred and fifty ton.[11] We went up anyway.

Now, we had a fellow by the name of Tom Colford. Tom was a man about two hundred and eighty pounds, and be God when we were to sign the articles Tom went over last to sign, and when he took the pen in his hand to sign he stopped.

He turned around to the captain and he said, "Captain, I don't think I'm going to sign," and the captain said, "Why?"

"Well," he said, "something is after struck me mind not to go on that vessel."

"Well, boy," the captain said, "please yourself. If something struck your mind not to go on the vessel, that's up to yourself."

He said, "I'm not going." So Tom didn't go.

So the captain got up the next morning and went to St. John's and he got two more. One of them was Tom Fillyard, and another by the name of Rich Kelly. Now they were two old sailor men, but the rest of us, myself and Jack Hearn, Tom Power and Fred Rossiter, this was our first trip ever on anything like that. We were just back and forth to the Labrador. We knew all about canvas and that, because you learn that going back and forth to the Labrador.

So we left Brigus and went down the bay. We had a beautiful evening. And just as we turned the cape the wind came up from the northwest and blowed a storm of wind. Anyway, it blowed so hard we had to run off the land and hove her to.[12] We was eight days running on that one side. It drove her across the Virgin Banks.[13] We were handier to them than he thought we was. There was an awful sea on and we could hear them breaking. Anyway, he runned her clear of them. Our canvas got all tore up. We had to use the mizzen for a storm sail. We lost all canvas.[14] It was old and rotten. They[15] were trying to run her as cheap as they could.

So anyhow, we took the wind from the northeast[16] and we runned towards Sydney. And when we got within two hundred and fifty or three hundred miles off Sydney, God, the wind came from the northwest again and it blew a storm of wind. So anyhow, we were lying to for two or three days, and by and by the captain says, "Boys," he says, "there's something wrong with this vessel, she don't seem to be handling herself the way she should." He said, "She's more dead than she used to be."

We went down in the cabin locker, and then we heard the water rising in the hold. There must be about four foot of water in her. We started to pump then. We couldn't free her. Now the Western Islands[17] were eight hundred miles away and Barbados was eighteen. We were out in the Gulf Stream then. He asked us what we wanted to do and we told him, "Skipper, we know nothing. Go where you like."

"Well," he said, "the Western Islands is eight hundred miles and," he said, "Barbados is eighteen hundred. Now," he said, "to run for the Western Islands you could make them and you may not make them and," he said, "you're running out of the steamboats' track.[18] But if we run for Barbados we're likely to run across a steamboat, and, if things get worse no doubt we'll have to abandon her."

179

So we went on and we never seen any steamboat. We went on and we got in the calms.[19] This is a place where there's no wind. You could be into them a day, you could be into them a week, or you could be into them a month. But we were fortunate we were only into them a week. Very hot weather there, too. Then we took the Northeast Trades. The Trades got heavier and she got worse, straining to try to carry on. Anyhow, she went down.

We were five hundred and fifty miles from Barbados when she went down. We carried canvas on her 'til the last minute. She hove out with a double-reefed foresail on her.[20] We had the two boats ready, 'cause we were expecting to have to leave her anytime. We had no grub to put in the boats 'cause we were only fitted out to go to Sydney. What we had left aboard, we had a case of cooked corned beef, and the captain brought that up on the cabin house and we never got a chance to get that. She hove out and we had to get in the boats before we had a chance to get it.

We never had a bit of grub, not a sip of water, and not a bit of tobacco—we never had a thing. That was a Wednesday, around the first of December, nine o'clock in the night. The wind was blowing hard and it was dark, and the last we saw of her her stern was just out of the water. The boat that we were in was twelve foot long. She was a jolly boat.[21] Myself and Tom Power and Jack Hearn was in that one. The others were in the big one, what they called the longboat. He was towing us so we wouldn't lose sight of one another.

But that night there was a rainstorm come on and a heavy squall of wind come with it, and we had to cut the tow line because we used to run ahead on the lop[22] and run across the towline, and when he'd bring up on us he could turn us over.[23] So we had to cut the line and let him go on. In the meantime we still had to go, 'cause we couldn't heave to. It was a big, heavy, short lop. So he went on.

The next morning we were still in sight of each other and we runned on with him about two miles ahead of us, 'cause he had a faster boat. Coming on dark he slacked off and we come up to him and he said, "We won't tow tonight. We'll keep in sight of each other with lights." See, he had a flashlight and we had flares.

Anyway, a rain squall came up and everything became pitch black, and when it was over we showed our light but we couldn't see his and, so he told us later, he showed his and couldn't see ours. When it came daylight and no sign of us, he thought we were after tripping[24] our boat, and we thought he was after tripping his. We had a sail on her then and just let her dodge on before the wind to see if we could see anything coming behind us. He thought we were gone, and we thought he was gone.

So anyway, we went on and on. Our rudder was gone and we had to steer with a paddle. We were sore trying to hold the paddle and keep the boat straight. We had a compass and we knew the course to steer all right, 'cause he told us.[25] We used to heave water over our heads, and our throats got dry, but we didn't get hungry at all. On the first of it we wanted water and that, but not afterwards.

We went on, and when we sighted land there was boats out catching flying fish and these were big centreboard boats.[26] We had a little signal on her where we saw a steamer that Sunday. She was a big two-stacker but she didn't see us. I suppose she didn't, she didn't come to our rescue, anyway. She went on. Those fellows[27] came up on side of us and asked if we wanted any help and we said no. Now we made a mistake, 'cause we didn't know where we were running to. We were running to the land all right, but what part of the land? We knowed it was Barbados Island, but what part of Barbados was it?

We didn't take any food from them because we weren't hungry. We were getting pretty weak, but we didn't know it.

181

We were a full week. She went down on Wednesday and this was the following Wednesday. Sometimes we did imagine things. You'd imagine sometimes there was something there, but you'd just imagine. When you'd come to yourself there was nothing there. I saw a woman, but whether it was my imagination or not, the woman came aboard the boat. She was there about a minute and she went again, that's all I know. And that day we made the land. When it came daylight, she was all dressed. To my imagination it was brown silk, that was the dress she had on, and she was there, stood up. I didn't see her face. She was back on to me. Whether it was my imagination, or whether the woman was there, I can't say. But if I had to say, I'd say yes the woman was there, I'd certainly say it, I certainly would.

So when we got down to this island, Barbados Island, God she was breaking heavy.[28] Now this was what they called the Cobblers Shoals, and that runned right along on the back of Barbados Island. This place was the proper graveyard years before that. An awful lot of vessels used to be lost there. And there was a lighthouse there and they had proper rescue sailors down in that lighthouse, and they put the flag up on the cliff but we didn't see the flag. They sent the men out, but we didn't see the men. But we trimmed[29] on down by the shore, and when they seen us trimming on down by the shore they went back again.

We went down to the end of the island. Well, there was no place to go in, only in over the rocks. So we said it was just as well to take a chance and go in over the rocks and take a chance on getting drowned there, just as well, as to go around the island and miss the island and getting drowned anyway. We knew we couldn't go much further.

We went in over the rocks and we went into a little cove about as wide as this room,[30] and be damn it there was a little fellow there. I dare say he was about six years of age, five or six years old, a little Negro fellow. And this little fellow came down and we said, "My son, what place is this?" "This is Barbados,[31] sir," he said, and with that he took off, and about five minutes after that here they comes, Negroes, all Negroes, men and women, and took the boat and hauled it up.

Now they had an old railroad track there, just the same as a railroad track. This used to be hauled by horses, and it was just the same as a flatcar with a roof over it, you know. There was a team of horses fast to that, and this is what they called the train. Now they had a real train there too, but that train usen't to go very often. Anyhow, we hauled it up across the track and we left it. Now they was to take us down to the station.

When we got to the land we gave out. We got hungry and we got weak, and they had to help us down to the station. Their station was only about three gunshots[32] from where we come in, in the boat. And we were expecting to go into a station the same as you would here.

When we got down there was an old fellow there. He was black. They was all black. We asked him where the station agent was to. He said, "I'm the station agent." And he had a pile of old boots all scattered around there—this house wouldn't hold them all. He was a shoemaker, used to mend boots, and this was his job although he was there looking after the station.

So anyhow, there was two horse police come, and detectives, and two doctors. The detectives was white, the horse police was black, and one of the doctors was white and one was black. They were all nice people, you know.

Now, they took our temperature and one thing and another, and they gave us half a glass of milk. So one of the horse police went on and came with three or four gallons of milk. Anyhow, that's all they give us, a half a glass and half a biscuit, half one of the soda biscuits. That's all they give us. Well in one yop[33] that was gone. We wanted more but the doctor said, "No." He said, "That's all ye're going to get for a while. Ye'll be all right. You know," he says, "ye may not feel it, but if you people eats any amount of corned beef now ye'll kill yereselves, and therefore we got to handle things now, just right."

So then the detectives took us in charge. Well they had to question us, where we was at, where we were going, what we had in, where we lost her, how far we went, what we went in, and was she gone out of sight when we last seen her. We said "no" to the last.. We told them all, we told them the truth anyway.[34] So that was all right.

By and by the doctor stepped in, 'cause they questioned us a lot, see. So one doctor says, "I think the best thing for you to do is to come back tomorrow morning and question them more then. We got to take those in charge now," he says, "and we understands their circumstances."

So they took us and went up to the courthouse with us. Now the courthouse was right on top of a big hill, and they got beds into a room in the courthouse for us. Three beds, a bed each, and the doctor stayed with us all night. And there were two horse police stayed with us all night, and one detective.

So every now and again the doctor'd take our temperature, maybe every half hour. He'd give us a little milk and a biscuit but he wouldn't give us anything heavy. So by and by the doctor says—see they were cute, you know[35]—he said, "Would ye care for something to drink?" Now he knew we couldn't drink. We said we wouldn't mind.

Now, see, the British Consul was standing[36] for all this and they knew it. So they sent off the two horse police to get some liquor. They bought[37] all kinds of liquor and put it on the table. Oh goddammit, the biggest kind of a table, and it was lined right off with liquor. Now they knew we couldn't drink. Anyhow, the doctor gave us a small drink of wine, that was all.

So we fell asleep, and when we woke we felt a lot better. So then he gave us something else to eat, and after awhile he gave us another small one to bring us around, see, to get something in our stomachs. So after a while he told the horse police, "Ye can go now and order a light breakfast." And the horse police said, "Yes, and what about ourselves?" "Oh yes," he says, "some for yourself and some for me and some for the detective." So anyway they come and put sixty dollars worth of grub on the table. We just sat down and ate[38] what we was allowed to eat. By and by he give us a drink of something a little stronger. I don't know what kind of liquor it was, but it wasn't wine.

So by and by the phone rang. When the phone rang this was the captain, Captain Sam Noseworthy in Bridgetown. Now see we were on the back of Barbados. We were eighteen miles from him. Now he still didn't know that we were landed, nor we didn't know that he had landed. But he happened to be into the drugstore. A fellow come in and was telling the drugstore fellow about the shipwreck crew that was after landing on the back of Barbados from a St. John's ship, 'cause that's what they called it.

So the captain called to see if it was us, and sure enough it was us. So now he says, "That's all right, I must send out a taxi for ye." So by and by here comes the taxi, and he come hisself in another taxi. So he bought lots of liquor, 'cause he was tickled to death because he done an awful thing to run away from us, see. What he shouldn't have done.[39]

So he said, "Now boys, when ye's ready, whenever ye like there's a taxi here to come in. I'm going back in the one

I come in." So he went back and this fellow stayed with us. So we had to go up then to the magistrate. Now we had to go up before him and tell him where we left, and what we had in, where we were going, and all kinds of every damn thing, all questions. Where was she insured to? Now see she happened to be insured in Bridgetown, Barbados, that's where she was insured to. There was lots of trials going ahead.

So anyway, when he had it all ready he said to the doctor, "Those men will be all right now. I'm going to send them back to Bridgetown, and the doctor over there will look after them."

So we come out and got in the car; and when we got in the car the magistrate come out to shake hands with us, see.

And when he shook hands with us the driver shoved his hand and said, "Hey, old-timer, take holt of that." He looked at him, he said, "What's wrong with you?" The magistrate said to him, "You're drunk." "No," he said, "I'm not drunk." Then he said, "Get out. I think now those men is after having it hard enough without being killed on the last of it."

"Now," he said, "you go back to your room and get a rest, and now," he said, "men, ye go up to yere room and stay there 'til that man gets sense enough to take ye back to Bridgetown."

So we went back to our room, and some of the liquor was there on the table. Those fellows had some of it took, see, but there was some left there. They were still there into a little room by theirselves. We went back to the room again and sot down and had a few drinks. It didn't take very much to knock us out. Anyway, so we got three parts drunk. This other fellow went out and had a nap. After he sobered up he woke up and he was all right.

So anyway, we left to go over to Bridgetown. "Now," he says, "what part of Barbados do you want to see?" We said, "We wants to see everything that's on the island." He said,

"That's going to take quite a while." We said, "We don't care how long it takes."

You'd see the car all flagged off with Union Jacks all around it. Every place we'd go there was a crowd on the corner to see the car coming with all the flags. They wanted us to stop to see what was going ahead. It wasn't a government car. It was a taxi, but see, the British Consul was paying for all of it. This is why they was so anxious to get all this liquor, 'cause the British Consul was paying for all that. They knew this. Of course we knew it too, but it was no odds to us anyway.

So we drove around Barbados and we went to the Sailors' Institute there, and we were there nine days. Now the way they used to cook there, they had the old pig iron, the very same they used to have in the olden days. The pig iron with the big boiler hung on the hooks and all that, the very same. We were well looked after there. We used to get a bit of money from the captain and go around and have a few drinks. The best drinks of rum were two cents a drink. Well, see, a shilling'd do you a long time in a place like that. It was all pounds, shillings and pence there. We used to have very good times there.

We were there nine days, and we came up on a boat called the *Canadian Otter*. There was a Negro sailor on it and he never seen a bit of snow in his life, didn't know what it was. And when we got off Halifax—that's where we was going to, in Halifax—it start to snow, and we used to tell him it was sugar. And he used to stoop down and pick it up on his finger and put it on his tongue. He'd say, "No, mon, dat's no sugar." He could talk English. We told him then. He said he often heard tell of it, but it was the first ever he seen.

So we got in Halifax and we came down from Halifax on the *Rodney*. The *Rodney* from Sydney was on the run at that time. They used to run back and forth from England and New York and St. John's, passenger boats. We stayed at the Navy League there in Halifax, that's where we stayed to.

The night before Christmas Eve she[40] come in there in the evening and we were supposed to come down on her, and she had a lot of sheet iron to land in Halifax. They start unloading about six o'clock in the evening, and the first sheet they come up with, be goddammed if it didn't get jammed in the hatch. They put it there so tight they couldn't get it back without burning it out of it, and the captain ashore. Now they didn't have too much to land there. When the captain come aboard he seen the hatch off her, and he seen the sheet of iron. He asked them the trouble and they told him. "Well then, whatever becomes of that sheet of iron," he said, "or however bad they want it, I'm eating my Christmas Day dinner home with my family in St. John's."

"So," he said, "put the hatches on her," and we left, and Christmas Eve about ten o'clock in the night we got in St. John's. He didn't slack on her at all,[41] and there was some wind coming behind her too. I know when we were coming down there was a good many coming from the States, and myself and Tom Power slept onside of two or three of them.

We woke in the morning and Tom says, "Did you have your breakfast?" and I says, "No I did not." He says, "Let's go look for some."

So be God we went out, and when we went out the two cooks was down there. One of them was a little short fellow, but he was fat and all you could see was the cap down over his shoulders. I went along to him and I said, "Cook, is there any chance of getting anything to eat?" He said, "Did you have your breakfast?" I said, "No, I didn't," I said, "to tell the truth, I didn't know there was any breakfast going."

"Well, boy," he says, "we sent a man through with a bell." "Well," I said, "we didn't hear it." And he looked at me and he said, "Can you eat your breakfast?" I says, "Yes we can eat our breakfast." "Well," he said, "men, if ye can eat yere breakfast, ye're the only two men in this ship this morning that can, including," he said, "the sailors that's on her. The sailors couldn't eat their breakfast here this morning," he said. "If ye're men enough to eat yere breakfast," he says, "I'm man enough to get it fer ye." That's the words he said, and he got our breakfast and we got in St. John's that night. He really forced on her.

When we got in St. John's it was frosty. We never had nar bit of clothes on us. Now at that time there was a fellow from Spout Cove[43] in the police force. His name was Henry Trickett. Myself and Henry was handy about the one age. We was good friends before he even joined the police force, but he was a policeman in St. John's. And he saw in the paper when we were leaving Halifax on the *Rodney*. He saw my name, so he came down. Now we were handy about the last there, 'cause you had to go through customs, see. And be God, anyhow, he come along and he says, "Andy, do you feel cold?" "Christ," I said, "how do *you* find[44] it?" I said, "I'm not cold, I'm chilled[45] 'cause I got nothing at all on me," I said. "This is a bit of clothes," I said, "we put on about three months ago and," I said, "it's still on us, half the time," I said, "soaking in salt water."

So he went up to the customs fellow and he told him about the three of us. "Tell the men," he said, "to go on, they got nothing anyway." "No," he says, "they got nothing, only a dirty shirt, that's all they got." That was all, so we come on.

We got on the train and got home about two o'clock that night, or two thirty. Plenty of moonshine and beer that night, Christmas Eve night. Everybody thought we were gone. They had the blinds down[46] and everything. My father had all the bit of money I made that summer on the Labrador. Now the priest had all that. Saying Masses for me and praying, he had

all that gone. I didn't have very much, a few cents I suppose.
I went to the ice that spring with old Captain Bartlett in the
Gulf. That was a hard year!

END NOTES

1 Actually, he means he went to the ice (i.e. sealing) during the spring following the shipwreck.

2 The merchant who owned the vessel hired Andy's father Bill to take the
vessel to the coast of Labrador in the spring and back to the island in the
fall. This was a common practice, for it was to the merchant's advantage
to transport his dealers and their crews and supplies to their various fishing stations. Bill Short was often hired for this purpose and was a very
capable seaman. Although he knew very little theoretical navigation, his
knowledge of the waters and coast on this 400- to 500-mile journey and
his experience as a seaman were such that he was well able to compen-
sate for any lack of formal training. Andy acquired some formal knowledge of navigation from other captains and was himself often hired to take
vessels to and from the Labrador.

3 The vessel belonged to the firm of J. W. Hiscock of Brigus, Conception
Bay.

4 The ship was the *Freedom* and was owned by A. S. Baird. With its three
masts and fore and aft rigging, this type of ship was referred to locally as
a "three-mast fore-and-after."

5 Here Andy is indicating that he did not know the captain's name at this
time, although he is interjecting the name into the story at this point.

6 Employment as a sailor in this context. It is also used to indicate
employment as a sealer or as a fisherman.

7 Newfoundland imported coal from Sydney, Nova Scotia.

8 Hoisting engines were gasoline motors which were often used on ships
during this period to hoist canvas and anchors.

9 Carbonear was the closest major port to Andy's home community of Kingston, and it was the business centre for that part of the coast.

10 At this time the rail line extended from Carbonear to Kingston, but it was later discontinued because it was extremely uneconomical. Andy is about to tell me how he went home and talked the matter over with his father, and he is explaining in advance why he was able to do this so quickly.

11 Here he wants to add force to his father's statement. A ship that size needed experienced deep-sea sailors, and if the captain was willing to hire men whose only experience had been on small Labrador schooners, then there was something very seriously wrong with the vessel. The ship's condition must be questioned even further, for this was a period of high unemployment in Newfoundland due to faltering fish markets and the declining seal fishery.

12 "To heave her to" is to turn the vessel about so that she is heading into the wind. In this position she has a better chance to withstand high seas and furthermore she won't be blown so far off course. They tied up all their canvas except the riding sail on the mainmast and the jumbo up forward, which were needed to keep the ship heading into the wind.

13 Dangerous shoals and rocks located on the Grand Banks.

14 However, they had extra canvas stored in the hold.

15 The owners.

16 The wind changed to the northeast, which was in their favour.

17 The Azores.

18 Sea traffic was considerably heavier on the route to Barbados than it was on the route to the Azores.

19 The Horse Latitudes.

20 The ship tipped on her side and went down. Apparently it happened very quickly, although they had been expecting it for some time. In a later conversation, Andy told me that the captain had a small dog which was the first to sense danger and jumped into the captain's lifeboat as the ship began to sink.

21 Andy later described the jolly boat as being a small boat about 12-14 feet long, which was used for "going ashore." The long boat was about 22 feet long and only used when goods were to be transported ashore or brought aboard.

22 In a later conversation, Andy described a "lop" as a small wave. In this case the lops were very close together.

23 If the small boat was on the tow line when it became taut, it could be capsized. In a later conversation, Andy informed me that their rudder was torn off by the tow line during this storm, and for the rest of the trip they steered with an oar.

24 If the boat turned side on to the lop it could "trip" or turn over.

25 It was no mean feat to maintain an accurate course over five hundred and fifty miles of empty ocean.

26 A deep-keeled sailboat which Andy says was called a sloop in Newfoundland in the "old days."

27 The fishermen from Barbados.

28 The sea.

29 They sailed on down by the shore.

30 On further questioning, Andy said that he steered the boat in over the rocks, and he added, "I was told about it since by people who were well acquainted with it, 'I suppose you're the only man that ever steered a boat in over the Cobblers Shoals without loss of life, the only man in the world.'"

31 They had landed in the St. John's District.

32 A gunshot is the average effective distance of a shotgun.

33 A yop is a quick continuous action whereby one bites and swallows in the one motion.

34 He is referring here to the question regarding whether the ship had actually sunk when they left the scene. This was important for insurance

purposes and also because an abandoned vessel which remained afloat could be a hazard to shipping.

35 "Cute" in this sense means shrewd or cunning, but not in the derogatory sense. In fact, in this context "cute" probably comes closer in meaning to the words "wise" and "intelligent."

36 Responsible for paying all costs.

37 In Newfoundland, "bought" is often used for "brought."

38 Ate is generally pronounced et, rhyming with get.

39 Andy and the men didn't think the captain had done an "awful thing to run (sail) away." What he means here is that the captain felt responsible and would have to face investigative inquiries, etc. if he lost three men under those circumstances. Furthermore, public opinion might easily hold him responsible, and stories of his not making a sufficient effort to locate the missing boat would be very hard to combat and could affect his career. Also, of course, in terms of human feelings, the captain must have been delighted at the news.

40 The *Rodney*.

41 He did not take his time. In other words, he forced the ship at her top speed.

42 The pitching and rolling of the ship was unusually severe.

43 A community near Andy's Home.

44 "Find it" in this context means "feel about the weather."

45 "Chilled" in this context means "extremely cold."

46 It was customary to draw window blinds for several days if a death occurred in the community. This practice is still common in some parts of the island.

The Wreck of the MV Monica Hartery

CLARENCE VAUTIER

The Wreck of the MV Monica Hartery

With the exception of a few last-minute preparations for Christmas Day, December 24, 1933, was a regular day in the fishing community of Rose Blanche on the southwest coast of Newfoundland. Several local fishermen were making a trip to check their herring nets in the vicinity of Rose Blanche Point, as they had done many times before. However, this trip turned out to be a little different.

As the men approached their nets, they saw something peculiar floating in the harbour entrance. As they came closer to the object, they discovered it was wreckage from a vessel, or more specifically, a section of decking from a schooner. This wreckage was floating just several hundred yards from the lighthouse on Cain's Island, leading the fishermen to conclude that the unfortunate crew likely found shelter in the lighthouse. They would soon discover that they were wrong.

The wreckage proved to be that of the MV *Monica Hartery*, a 73-foot coasting schooner, built in 1927 at Cape Broyle, Newfoundland, by Michael Hartery. The schooner operated in the coasting trade before being sold to Bowring Brothers in St. John's. After a short career with the Bowring firm, the vessel was again put up for sale and was subsequently bought by Levi Button of Lead Cove, Trinity Bay.

Mr. Button was a man of many trades. He had previously worked in New York as a steel rigger and in 1930, decided it was time to return home to Newfoundland. Sometime after returning home he became a policeman and later a businessman, establishing grocry stores in St. John's and Trinity Bay. From there, he bought the *Monica Hartery* and became involved in the business of coastal trading.

In the fall of 1933, Levi Button and his crew were chartered to carry gasoline from St. John's to Curling, Newfoundland. During one of these voyages, while passing the islands of St. Pierre and Miquelon on the south coast of Newfoundland, the vessel was battered by a storm that carried away her sails. With her canvas missing and a fierce storm raging, the schooner and her crew drifted helplessly in the Atlantic. Fortunately she was sighted by a passing schooner and was towed to Channel, Port aux Basques.

Upon arriving in port, the schooner's cargo was discharged and sent to Curling by train. The crew signed off and returned home. The sails were replaced and the vessel was moored at Channel for the winter. Shorty after she was secured for the season, Mr. Button met up with a local businessman who wanted to charter the *Monica Hartery* to bring a load of coal from Cape Breton to Channel. However, before Levi Button could accept the charter, he had to overcome a minor problem—finding a crew.

Mr. Button knew it wouldn't be easy to get a crew from the Trinity Bay area to make such a short trip so close to Christmas.

With this in mind, he decided he would have to find a crew in the Channel area. Levi Button was in luck. He met up with a local coasting captain, Alexander Keeping. Mr. Keeping had just finished coasting for the year with his father Theodore and brother George in the schooner *Joseph Earle*. He was well known in the area and in the coasting trade in general. He would have no problem finding a crew to make the short voyage for Mr. Button. In total, five crewmembers, including Captain Keeping and Mr. Button, would make the trip. If all went well, they would still have time to make it back for Christmas Day.

In the early evening of December 17, the *Monica Hartery* departed Channel and arrived at North Sydney the next day. Once in Cape Breton, the vessel was prepared to take on the load of coal, however, after it was loaded, the schooner was delayed in port for several days as a result of weather. Finally, on Saturday, December 23, the *Monica Hartery* and her crew departed North Sydney on their return trip home to Channel for Christmas.

Unfortunately for the crew and their families, they would not be together for Christmas. Sometime after the *Monica Hartery* left North Sydney, the vessel and her crew met their final destiny on or near the Newfoundland coast in the vicinity of Rose Blanche Point. Although most think the vessel ran aground, the events that led to the tragedy remain a mystery to this day. The only thing known for certain is that late on the night of December 23 and early morning December 24, the southwest coast of Newfoundland was ravaged by strong northwest winds and accompanying snow that resulted in near-zero visibility. From North Sydney the vessel would have to travel in a northeasterly direction to reach her destination at Channel. However, the strong northwest wind likely interfered with the vessel's intended course—the wind would have been slightly forward the vessel's beam—resulting in the vessel going off-course and subsequently wrecking off the Rose Blanche coast.

If indeed the vessel did run aground near Rose Blanche, abandoning the vessel would have been difficult. It would normally take the vessel a minimum of twelve to fifteen hours to get from North Sydney to either Channel or Rose Blanche, which meant the vessel would have been near Rose Blanche late Saturday night or early Sunday morning. This in turn meant that the crewmembers who were not on watch would likely have been sleeping, or tossing and turning in their cabins below.

If the fate of the *Monica Hartery* occurred suddenly in the blinding snow, the crewmembers below would have had very little time to dress properly for the poor weather, thus leaving their chances of survival slim. As for the crew who were standing on watch, they may have been thrown from the vessel when she ran aground. Even if they hadn't been thrown overboard, it is unlikely they would have been able to launch a dory without the help of rescuers, due to the extremely poor weather conditions.

Shortly after the local fishermen discovered the wreckage, the area was searched in hope of finding survivors. Unfortunately, there were none. The bodies of Alexander Keeping, Samuel Rideout, and William Strickland, along with small pieces of wreckage were found later in the day near Winging Point, near Rose Blanche Point. Their bodies were taken to the local lodge, where they were dressed, and placed in coffins made by the local residents. Mr. Keeping's father in the *Joseph Earle* later took the three bodies to Channel.

Three and a half weeks later, on January 17, 1934, a local fisherman from Rose Blanche was returning from fishing when he sighted something in the water. As he came closer to inspect it, he discovered it was a human body. It was taken aboard and brought into Rose Blanche and later identified as the remains of Levi Button. Mr. Button's body was taken to Channel on the SS *Glencoe* and sent back home via train. He was laid to rest on January 27, 1934. The body of Albert Neil was never recovered.

Calvin Pierce

Jim Wellman

Calvin Pierce

Calvin Pierce, Jr. is doing fine now. The 26-year-old native of Harbour Breton is married and living in St. John's. Calvin and his wife Sherry can't wait for the arrival of their first baby.

But, Calvin Pierce will never go fishing again. Not since the accident that claimed the life of his dad, Calvin Pierce, Sr., and his uncle, Hughie Snook.

Friday, May 10, 1996 started out as a typically cool spring morning in Harbour Breton. Although there were several small patches of ice in Northeast Arm, about five miles down the coast, Calvin Pierce, Sr. knew it was a good morning to go herring fishing. Calvin's brother Gordon, his brother-in-law Hughie, and his son Calvin, Jr. decided to join the 46-year-old fisherman for the day.

Fishing was good that morning, and the four men were soon on the way back to Harbour Breton with about 3,000 pounds of herring in their 19-foot speedboat.

By noon the southeast winds had freshened a little, but not much. When the four fishermen finished unloading their catch, Calvin decided that it was safe enough to go back to their bar seine for another load. Although the waves were getting higher with the strengthening winds, the experienced fisherman figured that things would be fine as long as they didn't overload the boat. Just before 2:00 P.M., the four were again on the way from Northeast Arm to the fish plant in Harbour Breton, this time with barely more than a half-boat-load of herring.

Calvin, Sr. kept the speedboat at a slow but steady pace as he steamed toward port on the western side of Northeast Arm. Mindful of the brisk winds, he kept the boat in the lee of the cliffs, about a quarter mile from shore. A little over one mile into the 4-mile trip back to port, a large wave struck their boat broadside, partially filling the front fish-well with water. As the salt water flushed forward to the front of the speedboat, the load of herring was carried along with it. With the bow weighed down to just inches above water, a second wave washed easily over the gunwales, completely filling the boat.

When the speedboat began to capsize and roll over, all four men were thrown into the water. Moments later, they were scrambling for safety on the overturned hull of the small vessel. As wave after wave swept over the boat, nearly washing the four into the ocean each time, Calvin, Jr. decided to leave the relative safety of the bottom of the speedboat and got back into the water. His plan was to try and keep the boat from tossing around in the waves, to make things more comfortable for his father and the other three men. Buoyed by his immersion suit, the young man managed to get the boat's painter (rope) under his feet for support as he stood in the water, tightly grasping the stem. As each wave approached, Calvin pushed and turned the boat in a way to minimize the impact of the waves when they struck. At the same time he was trying to manipulate the boat's movements, Calvin was also desperately trying to shed his rubber clothes and hip rubbers. The weight of the long rubber boots filled with water was nearly keeping him beneath the surface each time a wave washed over him.

Realizing that all four men would soon suffer the effects of hypothermia in the bitter cold water, Calvin, Jr. knew that something had to be done immediately. That's when he remembered the other, smaller boat they had left behind, tied to the bar seine. "I though that if I could get that small boat I could come back and then get the other three safely to shore," he says.

Not a strong swimmer, Calvin floated on his back and, using his best imitation of the backstroke he finally made it close enough to shore to crawl on his hands and knees to the beach.

Despite being safe on land, Calvin's worst nightmare was just beginning.

As he hurried to pull off his cumbersome immersion suit in order to walk and run faster, Calvin glanced out over the bay and saw his three relatives still clinging to the overturned speedboat. Wearing only wool socks, Calvin couldn't run on the jagged, ice-covered rocks, but he walked as fast as he could, his feet numb from the frigid water and below-freezing temperatures on land.

About halfway along the one-mile stretch of shoreline to the boat, Calvin faced another serious dilemma. The navigable part of the rocky beach ended where a steep cliff jutted out into the ocean. The only way to the other side was to climb over the cliff or swim around the headland. Even without boots, Calvin immediately chose to climb. Without an immersion suit, swimming was not an option for the young man.

On the other side of the cliff he was faced with yet another obstacle. A trench-like gorge extended all the way from the shoreline, as far inland as he could see. With the hillside heavily covered in thick brush and trees, it was nearly impossible to walk inland and then to the other side of the crevice. Calvin had just one option—he had to jump across the chasm.

Beating down bushes and breaking tree branches with his bare hands, Calvin made a narrow clearing long enough to get up a running speed before jumping. Backing up as far as he could, he mustered what strength he had remaining and ran, literally, for his life. He almost made it. Landing about two feet short of the top of the trench, he landed on a gravel slope. "All I can remember is my hands digging into the ground, and dragging myself up to the top," he says.

Finally, Calvin reached the beach where the small boat was moored about a hundred feet off shore. Looking out at the boat, Calvin realized he was faced with another nearly impossible challenge. Could he possibly swim to the boat without his floater suit to keep him safely above water? he wondered. Driven by anxiety and an overwhelming compulsion to rescue his father and his uncles, the young man knew there was only one thing to do. Calvin doesn't remember the swim, but he recalls that he was too exhausted and cold to climb over the side of the small boat once he got there. Finally, he pulled himself hand over hand around the gunwales to the stern, where he positioned the outboard motor at an angle whereby he could step on the propeller casing and push himself into the boat.

By the time Calvin made it back to the overturned speedboat, there was no one there. Suddenly, he noticed two men floating, lifelessly, near the shoreline.

"The exact details are hard to remember, but I knew by the way they were floating or something that my father and

Hughie were gone; that there was no hope for them, so I turned my attention to the third person, the one I couldn't see at the time." Running the boat around in circles just off shore from the beach, Calvin finally caught a glimpse of his uncle lying on the rocks. Afraid the engine wouldn't start again if he shut it off, Calvin rammed the boat in on the beach as he tilted the outboard motor and left it running with the propeller out of water.

Shouting and waving, Calvin ran along the shoreline, overjoyed to see his uncle Gord kneeling on his hands and knees. "He was dazed and frothing from the mouth, but I grabbed his pants and pulled on him until we both managed to get in the boat."

Afraid they wouldn't make it as far as Harbour Breton in the choppy seas, Calvin headed toward a cottage near the beach in Baldens Cove, about a half-mile away. Calvin remembered seeing the owner of the cabin by the shoreline earlier that day when he passed by the small cabin. Finally, for the fist time since the beginning of the nightmare, Calvin's luck took a turn for the better.

Stan Perry was still at his cabin that afternoon. Leaving his uncle Gordon at the cabin with Mr. Perry, Calvin wolfed down a tin of Irish Stew and started out on his last painful journey that day. Walking the half-mile path to the highway, the young man flagged down a passing car and hitched a ride to the RCMP station in Harbour Breton. The officer on duty recorded the time of Calvin's arrival at the detachment head-quarters as approximately 4:00 P.M.

Gordon Pierce made a full recovery, although he's still haunted by the memories of the ordeal. He still lives in Harbour Breton. Calvin Pierce moved to St. John's and vows he will never again fish for a living.

No one is absolutely sure why Calvin Pierce, Sr. and Hughie Snook left the overturned boat. They possibly decided that their best chance of survival in the bitterly cold water was to try and swim to shore, or perhaps they were washed off the swamped hull of the speedboat. An autopsy report determined that both Calvin Pierce, Sr. and Hughie died by drowning on their final fishing voyage.

Index